COOKING ON T

In this book a working mum sh
varied menu, give the kids their fa
dinner, even when the budget is s

Also in this series
CLOTHES FOR THE FAMILY
FOOD FROM YOUR GARDEN
FURNISHING ON A SHOE-STRING
HOLIDAYS ON A BUDGET
HOME-MAKING ON A BUDGET
HOUSE AND GARDEN MAINTENANCE
MAKING MONEY FROM HOME
RENOVATING FURNITURE
THE ECONOMY KITCHEN

COOKING ON THE BREADLINE

by

Jo Hatcher

Series Editor Jacqueline Dineen

THORSONS PUBLISHERS LIMITED
Wellingborough, Northamptonshire

First published 1978

ISBN 0 7225 0415 2

Photoset by
Specialised Offset Services Limited, Liverpool
and printed and bound in Great Britain by
Weatherby Woolnough, Wellingborough, Northamptonshire

CONTENTS

Dedicated to my faithful panel of
tasters, testers and bowl-scrapers:
My six beautiful children
Joanna, Caroline, Penny, Siobhan, Daniel
and Patrick

1

The Bare Necessities

Nobody taught me to cook. When I was a child my jobs were looking after the hens, bathing the younger children and keeping them out of mischief (or teaching them mischief), and doing the shopping – either with kids in the pram or on my bike at the nearest village shop one and a half miles away.

I did once try to cook something, but my father said: 'Who let her in the kitchen?' I only cooked baked potatoes in camp fires after that.

So, when I first married, I couldn't even boil an egg. But I bought a cookery book on the instalment plan which showed you how to lower an egg into boiling water and arrange it in an egg cup. It also explained things like 'roux' which I had always thought was a baby kanga.

But I did want to cook, so I taught myself. I didn't have any scales for a long time, but quickly got the hang of cutting a half-pound block of margarine in two to get four ounces, and each of those in half to get two ounces. And I divided a pound packet of sugar into cereal bowls to the same level to get four ounces. All you had to do was read the amount that was in the packet and divide accordingly. The family recipes that my mother gave me were usually in cups and spoonsful.

I have had to cook on the breadline for years, and have always been surprised at how much other people spend on food. Yet we have an interesting and varied menu and my six children are all horribly healthy and full of energy.

First attempts at cooking.

During the past few years when money was more plentiful, and frozen food and convenience foods were on sale in every shop, I think a lot of people began to forget about home cooking. But now 'convenience' foods are inconveniently expensive (and anyway they don't taste like the real thing), so we have to go back to the kitchen and cook the way our mothers and grandmothers did. Cooking is fun. Creating a dish is much more satisfying than opening a tin or a packet, or thawing out a block of stuff from the freezer shop. Being short of money doesn't depress me. It just brings out the mother of invention.

Variety of Recipes

We are far luckier than all those cooks who were struggling to feed their families during the last war. Holidays abroad and the many foreign restaurants that have sprung up in this country have introduced us to a greater variety of dishes. If you want to economize and feed your family well, you have a wide choice of Italian, Indian, French and Spanish recipes – and I have included our family favourites in this book.

When food was rationed, the population of Great Britain was never healthier. We had to make greater use of fruit and vegetables (which supply essential vitamins), and we couldn't eat too much – so we were all in better shape. Obesity is a problem in this country – even among schoolchildren. It is very rarely a glandular problem. It is more usually caused by the family's eating habits, and as the cook on budget, you can sort that one out.

The principles of successful catering on a budget seem to me to be 'Don't buy it – make it'.

Presentation is important. Always lay the table attractively and never apologize for your food. You can make meals more interesting by giving them a good name. How about 'Macaroni formaggio alla Josephina', instead of 'Sorry, kids, it's macaroni cheese again.'

Equipment

Cooking is a job, like any other, but it is also a form of art, and you do need some specialized equipment.

Of course you need a cooker, a sink, and a working surface. It is helpful to have a water heater, but you can manage with a large kettle. A fridge is useful, but you can get by with a cool larder – particularly if you have a marble slab on one of the shelves. If you can afford a deep freeze (one with shelves is easiest) then this will help you to save time and money as well.

I don't believe in cluttering up drawers, cupboards and work surfaces with electrical gadgets. The mixer my mother gave me was used twice and is now waiting to go to a good home. I find I just don't need electrical equipment. And if you have gadgets they need looking after, servicing, insuring and when they go wrong you have to get cross about it, and spend time and money trying to get someone to fix them. You stay in waiting for the man who never comes.

When I was cooking regularly for eight at every meal, and children haggled and wrangled over who was doing the washing up, I did buy a dishwasher. Even then there was trouble over who was going to stack, press the button and unload and put away. It used a lot of electricity, made a noise and left smears. When it went wrong I had to find a service engineer and he told me I should pay a regular £10 a year to cover breakdowns.

My washing-up bowl and mop have never broken down.

Keeping it simple, I use a wooden spoon, a rotary egg whisk and a sieve for most mixing and puréeing operations. I have been given various clever things like a cherry de-stoner and a gadget for making mashed potatoes into neat mounds, but I hardly ever use them and they lurk at the back of a drawer. A garlic crusher is useful, but ask yourself first if you are going to enjoy cleaning all those little outlets with a pin. You can always crush garlic with a knife.

What to Acquire

If you are setting up home have your mother or your mother-in-law's cast-offs and doubles, or look for most of what you need in junk and second-hand shops. My best heavy frying pan came from the scouts' jumble sale for a few pence. And look what's happened to that non-stick one someone gave me! It peeled. And finally turned back into an ordinary pan after a weekend of effort by an Italian student lodger. Luigi Pestaloni greeted me proudly: 'I cleana the panna. She was all burnta.' He had spent hours with a knife and brillo pad removing what he thought was burnt food.

So here is my basic list of kitchen utensils:

Saucepans with lids:

- 2 1½-pint size
- 1 old one for boiling eggs
- 2 3-pint size
- 2 8-pint size
- 1 chip pan

Frying pans:

- 1 for fish
- 1 for meat
- 1 for omelettes and pancakes

Kettle:

4 pints (electric if you like)

Cake tins
Bun tins (also used for Yorkshire puddings)
Sandwich tins (also used for flans, tarts etc.)
Loaf tins
Roasting pan (also used for cakes)
Baking tray
Paella pan with lid
Kitchen scales
Wall can opener (much safer than the stab-yourself variety)
Casseroles (cast-iron are best)
Pie dishes
Pudding basins
Large mixing bowl
Sieve
Collander (not plastic)
Tea strainer
Wooden spoons
Potato peeler
Vegetable knife (my favourite is ancient steel)
Knife sharpener
Fish slice
Perforated spoon
Rotary egg beater
Grater (old-fashioned metal sort is best)
1-pint measuring jug
Lemon squeezer
Container for cooking salt
Scrubbing brush for vegetables (old nailbrush)
Potato masher
Cake rack
Mincer
Refuse bin with lid

There is no need to buy dish clothes, oven cloths, tea towels, floor cloths or aprons. Make them all. Make yourself a long apron to wear when you're being glamorous in your long dress.

You do not need biscuit cutters – use glasses of various sizes.

Or a rolling pin – use a wine bottle.

You do not need to buy storage jars or tins. When you're

shopping, look for coffee sold in jars with screw-on lids. Use biscuit tins for storing cakes and biscuits and homemade pasta.

You can make a chopping board and breadboard from hardwood offcuts. I use a large flat melamine plate as a chopping board which means no juice is wasted and it is easy to wash.

When you buy utensils look for good solid quality. Do not buy plastic gadgets or a plastic collander. Plastic snaps or melts.

There are a few non-essentials which are fun to have when you can afford them. For instance: animal biscuit cutters, fancy flan tins and individual flan tins. An icing gadget will help you to decorate your cakes more expertly. Again, buy a metal one.

Sad story. I saved for weeks to get one and the baby threw it out of the pram in front of a passing lorry. Never mind, I saved up again.

You will also need a large preserving pan. I use a giant vitreous, enamelled, cast-iron casserole. This is useful for enormous stews, for making jam, pickles, chutneys and for mixing large quantities, such as Christmas cake or the dough for the week's supply of bread.

Food Supplies

It is best to have a store cupboard in which you can keep a duplicate of every item of non-perishable food that you use. Keep the packets in actual use in cupboards in the kitchen grouped according to type.

In my scheme for cooking economically I have the following in my store cupboard, which gives me a feeling of security and saves time, temper, panics and running down to the late-opening shop with the inflated-inflated prices:

- Flour:
    - plain
    - self-raising
    - wholemeal
    - cornflour
- Sugar:
    - dark brown soft
    - granulated
    - demerara

caster
icing
glucose

Pasta:
macaroni
spaghetti
lasagne (but you can make this)
other fancy types

Pulses:
lentils
split peas
red beans
haricot beans

Cereals:
oats
pearl barley
breakfast cereals
rice (round and long grain)
semolina

Drinks:
coffee (try to get your vistors on to tea)
tea
cocoa
oxo

Also:
groundnut oil
vinegar
dried fruit
gelatine

Plus a collection of herbs (but you can grow these), spices, curry powder, dried yeast, pepper, salt, flavourings and cooking aids like cream of tartar and bicarbonate of soda.

The only tinned goods are tinned tomatoes, syrup, treacle, and dried milk (the latter for emergencies when you find you have to make a sauce or pudding and it doesn't look as if there'll be enough milk left for breakfast).

In the fridge I have:
milk

margarine
lard
a bowl of dripping
cheese in plastic bag
eggs

If you have a deep freeze, this can be stocked with other people's gluts of fruits, *puréed*; their gluts of vegetables, blanched and stored in polythene bags; and cheap offers from the deep-freeze shop: mince, sausagemeat and perhaps a turkey bought half-price just after Christmas.

Also, your own bread, rolls, casseroles, pizza, quiche and other home-made savouries, apple crumble and other puddings, and any special offers in the perishable line that you have snapped up in the supermarket, such as butter, margarine, lard.

Keep your vegetables in a dry place, and take them out of plastic bags if they are sold wrapped this way. A wire vegetable rack will do, but I keep mine in wooden boxes with a piece of newspaper in the bottom. If you put down several layers of paper, you only need to take out the top one with the dust on it when you clean them out

Salad vegetables should be washed and stored in the bottom of the fridge. You can also store any surplus fresh fruit here.

So now, with a squirrel's store like this, you are ready to produce a meal at any time.

2

Cutting the Cost

You can save on gas and electricity in the following ways:

Don't buy a stove with automatic pilot lights. And if you have one, get the pilots turned off. Use tapers to light the gas stove instead of matches if you have a water heater with a pilot in the kitchen. Make your tapers from slices of cereal packet.

You don't need a self-cleaning stove that heats up and burns the dirt off. That costs big money.

If you must have a pilot light on your stove, leave a pan or kettle of water over it at night to heat water for the breakfast washing up.

De-furr the kettle and don't put more water in it than you need at a time.

Use a pressure cooker, or twin saucepans. Fill up the oven by careful planning. Turn the gas or electricity off under a pan of vegetables halfway through the usual cooking time. They will finish cooking in the hot water (taking a little longer than usual, of course). Cut vegetables into small pieces, cook together when possible, keep pan lids on and use only as much water as is really necessary.

De-frost fridges and deep freezers regularly.

Remember to turn off the kitchen light when you leave the room.

Saving When Shopping

'Don't buy it – make it.' Remember that when you go shopping and you are bound to save money. If you buy anything that has been processed, prepared, cooked, tinned, bottled, or packaged extravagantly you are paying for the processing, labour, wrappings and advertising. In supermarkets you will usually find that 'own brand' is cheaper than the same product under a 'household name'.

Buy larger sizes whenever possible, but even so, watch out. You may find there is no saving on a large size, and I have even found occasionally that a large tin of tomatoes is the usual price, while smaller tins are on 'special offer'.

Equip yourself with a small accounts book (or make one from the backs of last year's Christmas cards). Make a note of everything you buy, and the cost. In this way you cannot just forget your extravagances!

At the other end of your book make a list of all staple items and use this as a check list when you make out your shopping list.

Choosing Your Shops

To find out where to get the best value for money, detail various members of the family to note down the prices of all your usual purchases in different shops. This can be a sort of competition for the children, hunting for the cheapest. Watch out for special offers, but while you're in a particular shop buying them up, don't automatically get the rest of the shopping. The special offer is often a lure, and you may find your saving on it completely lost in the odd pennies on this and that.

If you find the prices in a shop which gives stamps are competitive, do some of your shopping there. Then you can exchange the stamps for groceries or a present for the house when the books are full. Some shops give double stamps mid-week.

Shopping mid-week is easier than at the weekend. You won't catch me in any supermarket on a Saturday! Midweek the shops are less crowded and you can get round more easily. You don't waste time queueing at the check-out in the supermarket and being pushed by the impatient shopper behind you while you're trying to pack your bags. Nor does your baby have so much time to snatch the sweets, so cruelly placed within his reach.

Don't bother to put anything into a paper bag at the check out unless it really needs it. You'll only have to waste time and energy unpacking it when you get home.

Make (of course) a couple of strong shopping bags. Then you won't be caught out and have to pay extra pence for a plastic carrier bag (which doesn't last long anyway). Take your broken plastic carriers with you to wrap wet fish, dripping meat or muddy vegetables.

Another tip in the supermarket: if something has gone up in price, look at the back of the shelves to see if any packets are still marked with last week's price.

Try small grocers' shops (the smarter the better) for bacon scraps and dried ends of cheese which are perfect for cooking.

Markets

Markets are a good place to buy your fresh vegetables, but take a walk right along before buying. You may find the stalls farthest from the main road are selling even more cheaply than the first ones you pass. Stalls have a quick turnover and their produce is fresh. If you go late in the day, particularly on a Saturday, there are plenty of bargains as stallholders have to get rid of their perishables. This is also the time to ask for cabbage leaves and so on if you have guinea pigs or rabbits. If your child has a pet, suggest he chats up the local greengrocer and make an arrangement to collect his trimmed off leaves.

Market vegetables and fruit have not spent so many hours or days being graded, washed, packed in plastic covered trays and labelled, so are usually fresher. Also, it does seem that stallholders accept the fact that you're going to shout if they do try to sell you a rotten pear, and they replace it without too much fuss. They don't want to lose their reputation in front of those other customers.

You'll often find stalls in the market selling eggs, cheese and other farm produce more cheaply than you could buy in the shops. And sometimes there are stalls selling tinned, bottled and packaged goods at way below shop prices. This is because their overheads are far lower than any shop. But don't accept bent tins.

Complaining About Bad Quality

If ever you find something wrong with any food you have purchased, either return it to the manufacturer or complain to the shop. I know a girl who received the occasional gift of a new product after complaining about the state of some processed cheese. The manufacturers replaced her cheese with interest, and kept her informed of their future products, actually asking for her opinion of them.

In the days when I bought pies, I complained about one that had mould on top when I unwrapped it, and a very apologetic representative came from the firm and presented me with two pies and four pounds of sausages!

I bought some frozen beans once and they were grey so I returned them to the manufacturer with a surprised letter.

Next day the phone rang, and an aggressive voice said:

''Ere, are you the lady complainin' about beans?'

Crumbs. If that was the complaints department, it didn't look as if I was going to get any satisfaction. I said defensively:

'Yes. They were grey.'

'Yeah,' said the irritated voice. 'I can see that. This is Kilburn sortin' office. Wish you'd packed 'em better. The parcel's bust open and drippin'.'

Anyway, he must have re-packed them and sent them on their way, because I received an apologetic letter and a postal order refunding my money and postage.

Farm Shops

If you're out in the country, watch out for farm shops and notices on people's gates. Prices are lower because there are no middleman profits.

Farms and orchards often invite you to 'Pick your own', which is also worthwhile, and you can make it a day out for the family, or a camping weekend at the same time. Maybe the kids can have their first taste of slave labour, too. Mine went off strawberries completely for weeks after our first expedition. But then I think they were putting one in their mouth for every five in the bucket! However, picking your own is a good way of stocking up the freezer or getting enough fruit cheap to make jam. You can store

Their first taste of slave labour.

apples in a cool, airy cupboard.

You may like to investigate bulk buying in your area. The only snag to this is that you have to have transport and capital, and you may find you don't actually save much money, although it is certainly convenient to have a well-stocked store cupboard.

Don't Be Brainwashed

When you make out your shopping list, do not be brainwashed by your children or the television ads. They're probably both trying to persuade you to buy gimmicky or over-priced products that you don't really need. Just because your eight-year-old's friends are all eating Sammy Squirrel's Muesli which costs a fortune, there is no reason to stop making it yourself from the equally nutritious ingredients bought separately and far more cheaply. Of course, there does come the odd occasion where you may find it reasonable to buy the same cereal for several weeks because your child is collecting free stickers or plastic animals. 'Someone must have eaten the penguin that was supposed to be in this packet, Mum. We didn't find it.'

Look through your collection of money-off coupons (snipped from magazines and the ones that have popped through the letter box) and discard all the rubbishy ones, like Dame Katy's Plastic Honey Pudding or Colonel Jumbo's Cardboard Crust Jungle Pie.

Don't Buy It – Make It

Remembering the principle of 'don't buy it – make it', there are dozens of things you need never buy – anyway, they don't taste as good as home-made. You don't get the compliments and praise that are the rewards of a good cook, either. What husband has ever said: 'Darling, you have opened that tin of barbecued chicken exquisitely and re-heated it so beautifully. I love you.'

When I started playing at making my own pasta, one of my children said he thought he didn't like ravioli, but now he did. He had only ever eaten the tinned variety before because he was famished.

So don't buy: ready-made frozen, packet or tinned meals (this includes soup), frozen pastry, packet puddings, cake mixes, pastry mixes, bread mixes, cakes, biscuits, jam tarts, puddings, trifles, trifle mixes, instant puddings, mousses, yogurt, jelly, bread, buns, rolls, breadcrumbs, tea bags, beefburgers, jams, chutneys, pickles, tomato sauce, salad cream, tinned or frozen fruit or vegetables – unless any of these are a ridiculously priced special offer. Don't waste money on meat pies and it's cheaper to make your own skinless sausages. Make your own crisps, potato sticks, toffee and fudge.

Buy washing-up liquid by the gallon, half fill your squeezy bottle and top up with water. Buy scouring powder from the market or a supermarket own brand. Don't buy kitchen towel rolls, greaseproof, jam pot labels and covers (see Chapter 7).

Recycling

Buy kitchen foil but wash it, hang it up to dry and use it over and over again. The same applies to plastic bags. Save every paper bag and piece of greaseproof paper. Paper bags are useful for rubbish, for draining fried food and for sandwiches. Use the greaseproof from cereal cartons for your baking. Plastic bags are useful for storing oddments in the fridge, and if you keep one by you when you're working in the kitchen, you can shove your floury hand into it to save mess when you answer the phone or the door, or open a cupboard.

When you buy things like coffee look out for jars with plastic screwtops to use later for preserves, pickles and storage. Buy ice-cream in a plastic container that you can use afterwards as a storage box in fridge, cupboard or freezer, and for packed lunches.

Cheaper Alternatives

Avoid any item that is temporarily over-priced. Don't just moan and pay up. Think of something you can buy instead. For instance, when potatoes are very expensive, use recipes where the bulk is provided by pasta, rice, pastry or suet crust.

If lettuce is expensive, eat dandelion leaves and cabbage hearts. (Don't ever pull up a dandelion again thinking it is just a wicked weed. It is a food.) Chinese lettuce may be cheaper than white cabbage. We're lucky. There is great variety in the vegetable line as we become more and more international.

When you're shopping you may often see things like bananas with black skins being sold off cheaply. Buy them to eat or make into something immediately. They're usually perfectly all right inside. The same applies to avocado pears and 'over-ripe' melons. These two are at their best when really ripe.

Washed vegetables don't keep as long as unscrubbed because their protective layer has been removed. If you do buy root vegetables in plastic bags, let them out the minute you get home or they will sweat and deteriorate more quickly.

Grow your own herbs in pots and window boxes, and turn part of your garden over to vegetables, or rent an allotment. You can grow cabbages and so on among the flowers. Start your seed in boxes on the window sill at the appropriate time and then you won't have to pay for bedding plants.

If you haven't a garden, you can still grow tomatoes in boxes and tubs on outside windowsills or a balcony.

Milk

A pint a day for children is essential, but you can cut down on its use in cooking by using half water, half milk in sauces, custards, puddings and so on. If it goes sour, don't throw it away; use it for sour milk scones or make cream cheese.

Meat

Find a 'friendly neighbourhood butcher'. There are still some, and if you chat him up he'll do wonders for you in the way of advising you which is the best bargain this week, and in supplying you with the cheaper cuts of meat and all the useful parts of an animal which were traditionally part of the weekly menu in past lean times. I doubt if you would find half a pig's head in any supermarket to make brawn, for instance, but your butcher can get you one specially.

You can save a lot of money on the meat bill by using 'old-fashioned ingredients'. You may not be used to dealing with them, but it's worth having a try. Your family may not be keen on the idea of eating 'pig's head', so you will have to be subtle/crafty when preparing it, and most definitely call it 'brawn' when you produce the finished dish.

Just because you're watching your budget, you don't have to feel deprived. There'll be money over for the occasional treat in the way of food. And it *will* be a treat.

Your family's health depends on the food they eat. They will be fit and full of energy if you make sure they eat foods containing protein – eggs, cheese, pulses (things like beans and lentils), fish and meat. Meat is expensive and so is fish, but the other foods in that list provide just as much valuable protein. Everyone needs carbohydrates, which are provided in potatoes, bread, rice, flour and pasta. And essential vitamins are found in fresh fruit and vegetables. Most of us take too much sugar, so try to wean those members of the family who are three-spoons-a-cup greedies gradually down to a more reasonable one teaspoon or none at all. Milk is an essential source of calcium, and growing babies and children must have their pint a day. Most of us also have become used to eating too many fatty foods, or plastering our bread with butter. Don't serve too many fry-ups, and substitute margarine for butter. Ordinary block margarine is cheaper than the soft, easy-spreading variety.

The age group that needs the most calories are boys and girls who are growing fast – between the ages of eight and eighteen. They really do need as much food as an adult man, or more. They're not being greedy – they're burning it up. But try to discourage sweet and chocolate snacks. Fruit or raw carrots keep hunger pains at bay in a more healthy way. The sub-teenager or teenager who drinks water instead of sucking coke or fizzy drinks from a can won't have the embarrassment of spots.

3

Granny Used to ...

Our grandmothers and great-grandmothers cooked with the minimum of waste, and very economically, from necessity. And it was the natural thing to do. They had never heard of 'convenience' foods, deep freezes, ready-made meals or strawberries flown by jet out of season. If they wanted strawberries at Christmas time, they made sure they bottled them in the summer when they were cheap.

We can save a lot of money on our housekeeping by doing just what they used to do. So here is Granny's ABC.

Apples She used them to bulk out stews, chopped them up in the salad, puréed and bottled them, and dried them in rings. She cooked up the peelings and cores, put them through a sieve and made apple jelly, or put chopped mint into the jelly and served it with the joint.

Bones and carcases She always boiled them up in her stock pot.

Bread She made her own and kept it fresh in a bread crock. Sometimes she bought yesterday's cheap from the baker. She baked crusts and heels of bread on a tray in the oven, crushed it into crumbs and stored it in glass jars. She fried up inch squares of stale bread and served it up as croutons in the soup. She made it into Bread Custard, or Bread'n'Jelly. She used it for Apple Charlotte, Queen of Puddings, Summer Pudding, Bread Soup, Bread and Butter Fritters, Crispy Cheese Fingers. And even the baby's chewed crusts were mixed up in the dog's or cat's dinner to make it go further. She encouraged the birds to her garden and called to them as she scattered the crumbs from the bread crock.

Cream She took the top of the milk and left it to stand in a bowl. Then she re-skimmed it, and there was cream. She put a dob of it on the home-made raspberry jam on her home-made scones.

Cake She always made it, but she did buy stale cakes at the baker and used these for trifles and puddings.

Dandelions She put the young leaves in salads or sandwiches, cooked the outside leaves like greens and also made dandelion wine.

Dripping She saved all the fat from roasting a joint and we had it on toast or bread.

Dumplings She filled us up with them.

Eggs She kept hens and grew her own eggs. She preserved them in a bucket of Waterglass. If there were no eggs she used this substitute in cakes and puddings: For each egg left out – 12g ($\frac{1}{2}$ oz.) margarine, 2 tablespoonsful flour, 2 tablespoonsful milk, $\frac{1}{2}$ teaspoonful baking powder.

Elder bush She steamed the young leaves and they tasted like asparagus, and made the flowers into tea or wine. She made the berries into jelly, used them in pies and made them into wine.

Flowers She always had a jug of them in the kitchen, smelling and looking pretty.

Faggots The wooden sort she gathered on her walks. The edible sort she made.

Fish She made a little go a long way in a creamy fish pie. She served little pieces of cod in a creamy sauce, piped round with mashed potato in a scallop shell.

Goulash Granny turned an ordinary stew into a spicy goulash with paprika.

Hens Of course she grew her own, and the postman wrung their necks when they ceased to be productive. But as they were family friends, we ate the neighbours' hens and they had ours.

Hay She lined a wooden box with hay, and often finished stews off in it.

Herrings She had dozens of ways of serving them, rolled in oatmeal; boned and simmered with herbs, then she added gelatine to this fish stock and served them up cold with salad.

Icing When she felt creative, she decorated her ordinary weekly batch of biscuits with flower and animal patterns. Just for fun.

Jam She made it from any fruit or vegetable in season – carrot, marrow with ginger, pumpkin and all the usual fruits. She didn't throw away the scum, but put it in a jam dish and served it for children's tea.

Kitchen garden She had one with a giant rhubarb tree (we never saw the elephant who was supposed to live in it), all manner of herbs, angelica (which she candied), and a hedge of lavender, and another of parsley. She dried the herbs in paper bags hanging from the kitchen airer.

Ketchup She made it. It didn't keep long, but it didn't have to because it went so fast.

Lemons If she wanted a squeeze of juice, she just pierced the skin. She always grated the rinds and put the gratings in a screwtop jar. She dried what was left and used it to light the range.

Granny made her own cream cheese.

Lettuce 'The lettuce are bolting again,' she announced. She stewed the outside leaves like any green vegetable, and we ate the heart. She sowed a few lettuce seeds each week.

Margarine She used it instead of butter. And you either had margarine and jam, or just butter on your toast – 'Or you can't really taste it, dear.'

Milk She showed us how to put the top of the milk in a screwtop jar and shake it and shake it and shake it and shake it until it became blobs of butter. She used half milk, half water in sauces and custards. If it went sour she used it in sour milk scones, and if a whole pint had gone really sour and junketty she put a cloth over a bowl, poured it into it and hung the cloth bag up to drip. Result: cream cheese, sometimes livened up with chopped chives.

Mustard She kept it fresh by mixing it in a small paste jar, adding a little water when she cleared the table and putting the lid back on the jar tightly. She said Mr C. made his fortune from the dried mustard in people's mustard pots.

Mushrooms She looked for them in the fields, with us to protect her from the cows. She dried them for out of season use.

Nettles She put on her gardening gloves and gathered them. She served the young ones as a green vegetable or as soup.

Onions She used the sprouting tops in soups and salads. She strapped half an onion on her chilblain.

Oatmeal She used it to thicken the stew or soup.

Oranges She made fresh orange squash and candied the peels. She made her own marmalade.

Oddments Savoury leftovers went into the soup; sweet into a mystery dessert in a fancy dish.

Potatoes She made potato cakes and used potatoes in a hundred different ways – baked, boiled, smashed, chipped, sliced to decorate the mince.

Paté She made it from chicken livers or lamb's liver, adding her own herbs.

Parsnips She cooked them and mixed them with potato, made them into patties, fried them and served them with green vegetables and carrots.

Rabbits She grew them.

Radishes She had a continuous supply all summer, by putting in a few seeds each week. She stewed the green leaves.

Rose petals She crystalized them and used them to decorate the christening, birthday and wedding cakes.

Suet She bought it from the butcher, for suet puddings, lardy cake, dumplings and suet crust.

Seeds She collected the seed heads from her herbs and flowers, and dried them in paper bags.

Sweets and toffee She made them.

Tomatoes She made them into chutney and tomato sauce. She puréed and bottled them.

Tea She always served tea instead of coffee, in ordinary cups in the morning and dainty china in the afternoon. It was real tea, kept in a caddy. 'No, I don't buy tea bags. It is such a bother snipping them open, dear.'

Teatime It was bread and jam (two sorts), and cakes and biscuits and buns, to fill us up, so we only needed a light supper.

Ugly 'No one is really ugly,' she said. 'If you get enough sleep and fresh air and drink lots of water, you won't get spots and you'll have rosy cheeks. And if you try always to be good and kind, you'll be happy, dear.'

Violets She searched them out in the spring and crystallized them as cake decorations.

Watercress Granny found it in the streams, and we waded in our wellingtons to pick it. But she said, 'Mind now, never gather it from a stream in sheep pasture.'

Xmas Xmas started early with the making of sweet mincemeat, the cake and the puddings.

Yolks She kept egg yolks fresh by putting them in a cup (without a handle) and covering them with a little water.

Zizz Granny always made sure she had a rest in the afternoon. Then she changed and did something quiet and creative like a little gardening, or her embroidery. That was her 'thinking time' too.

Granny never wasted anything, and she had ways of coping with kitchen disasters.

If a sauce went lumpy, she put it through a sieve.

If curry turned out too hot, she put more potato in it.

If the soup was burning, she very quickly poured it into another pan, before it got any worse.

She always saved her butter wrappings to use when greasing baking and cake tins, or to lay on the baking tin before she put the biscuits on it.

When she made doughnuts, she just pushed a hole in the centre, so nothing was wasted.

She put a piece of uncooked macaroni in the centre of her pies to stop the juice pouring out of the sides as they cooked.

She put a teaspoon of salt in the egg water to stop shells cracking. You can safely seal a cracked egg with sellotape nowadays.

Did you know that if you dip your knife in boiling water before slicing hard-boiled eggs, it will stop the yolks from crumbling?

Still talking of eggs – if you beat the whites first with your whisk, and then beat the yolks, you won't have to wash your whisk.

When you make custard, take a short cut. Put the powder and sugar in the saucepan, cream with a little cold milk, then add the rest of the milk and boil until it thickens. That way you don't use an extra bowl.

If you want your jelly to set quickly, melt it in a little hot water, and then top up with cold, or ice cubes.

Food From Wild Plants

There isn't room in this book to give you details of all the plants and fruits that are growing wild, and which make good eating for nothing. If you're keen enough you can find books specializing in recipes using them.

But here are two which you might like to try.

Don't say 'Ugh!' before you've tried them. Stinging Nettle Soup does *not* sting the tongue and is absolutely delicious. We have it quite often. I met an Irishman once who told me that he and his five brothers and sisters lived on stewed nettles, potatoes and eggs for months when his mother was widowed at twenty-six and had no money at all.

Nettle Soup

225g ($\frac{1}{2}$ lb) nettle tops
1 small onion
Knob of butter
$\frac{1}{2}$l (1 pt.) stock
Salt, pepper, nutmeg
1 tablespoonful top of the milk

Wear plastic gloves to wash leaves and remove stalks from the nettles. Peel and chop the onion and fry in the butter. Add nettles and toss for 2 minutes. Add stock and simmer for 20 minutes. Put through a sieve, return to pan. Heat, season and add milk just before serving.

Elderflower Fritters

2 dozen elderflower clusters
2 eggs
Salt
275ml ($\frac{1}{2}$ pt.) milk
1 teaspoonful butter
100g (4 oz.) flour

Remove flower stalks, wash and shake dry. Beat eggs, mix in salt and butter (or margarine). Add flour and milk to make a smooth batter. Dip flowers into the batter and fry in deep fat until golden brown. Serve sprinkled with sugar.

4

Breakfasts and Packed Lunches

Gone are the days when we could afford a fry-up of bacon, eggs, tomatoes and fried bread for breakfast every day. The bacon has priced itself off the table, and tomatoes are often expensive, except when you're harvesting your own.

However, perhaps it is a good thing. Fry-ups are fattening and often lie heavy on the stomach. No one should start their day without breakfast. Not you or the children. Lack of early morning nutrition makes one accident prone, and dopey at school or work.

Children and adults will go off perfectly well nourished and fuelled to last until lunch time on the following:

Cereal with sugar and milk
Home-made bread with margarine and home-made jam or marmalade
Milk or tea to drink
An apple or orange or half a grapefruit.

Vitamin C has been proved to be important in helping the body to resist cold and flu germs. In an experiment at the school my eldest children attended, each child was given an orange a day, and colds and flu were dramatically defeated. The only children out of the 400 who suffered from them were the ones who gave their oranges to friends.

Your children may stick the apple or orange in their pocket for mid-morning break – but that is better and less expensive than a bag of crisps. Anyway you're going to make your own crisps from now on.

Make your own muesli from ordinary porridge oats (buy them in plastic bags at the supermarket, not in a cardboard pack which works out more expensive). Add a few sultanas, chopped apple and nuts if you have them.

If you family *must* have something cooked, there are alternatives to that overpriced bacon.

Make your own sausages, potato cakes, kedgeree. Wartime mock egg, and fish cakes.

Oatmeal Sausages

450g (1 lb) sausagemeat
75g (3 oz.) suet
225g (8 oz.) oatmeal
1 small onion
425ml (¾ pt.) stock or water
teaspoon sage or mixed herbs
salt and pepper

Fry the chopped onion in a little fat, add stock, shredded suet and bring to the boil. Sprinkle in oatmeal, sage and sausage. Cook for ¼ hour. Season. Turn out on a plate to cool, then shape into sausages, brush with milk and roll in crisp breadcrumbs (your own). Fry to crisp the outside.

Potato Cakes

Use mashed potato, mixed with just under half the weight of flour. Season. Roll out ¼ inch thick and cut into rounds with a glass. Fry.

Kedgeree

50g (2 oz.) rice
175g (6 oz.) cooked fish
35g (1½ oz.) margarine
1 hard-boiled egg

Cook rice, mix in fish and fat and stir in pan over low heat until really hot. Serve with chopped hard-boiled egg on top.

Wartime Mock Egg

Make a batter from flour, milk and water. Cut a tomato in half and dip in the batter. Lift out on a big spoon, keeping round side up, and fry in hot fat. The tomato shines through, looking like the yolk of an egg.

Fish Cakes

100g (4 oz.) cooked fish
1 teaspoonful chopped parsley
225g (½ lb.) cooked potatoes

Mix up potatoes, parsley and fish. Stir in a little milk if necessary. Make into cakes with floured hands. Fry until light brown on both sides. Serve with fried parsley.

Packed Lunches

You will find it is a lot cheaper to take your lunch to work. You won't waste time waiting to be served or queueing, and you won't have to moan about prices and quality. Some schools allow children to bring a packed lunch, and mine always take theirs to the Play Centre in the summer holidays.

But a packed lunch does not mean sandwiches every day. We could go back to the ancient idea of a roly-poly pud in a cloth, with meat and vegetables one end and jam or fruit the other!

If you buy ice-cream, buy it in plastic containers. They make very good lunch boxes, and my children take something to drink in a half-pint screwtop bottle. The 'No deposit. No return' bottles are useful, so as you've stopped buying tonic water, beg them off rich

Tie on the cutlery.

friends. Don't buy fizz, coke or crisps any more. Buy orange or lemon squash by the 2 litres in the supermarket.

Some of my suggestions do need a spoon or fork. Make a hole at one end of the box and tie the spoon on a string. Then it will return with the lunch box and the child. Write their name and school in felt tip on the box lid and bottom.

This is what my family expect to find in their lunch boxes: pizza, quiche, chicken breast fried in breadcrumbs, Cornish pasties, hard-boiled eggs, Scotch eggs, sausage rolls, three-decker sandwiches. French bread with cheese and chives, a small carton of mixed salad (I make a big bowl of this and keep it in the fridge; you'll find the ingredients listed in Chapter 9), raw carrot or fresh fruit, apple turnover or any of the following puddings in a screwtop jar – orange mousse, jam blancmange, jam jelly, fresh fruit salad. If you have somewhere in the office to heat soup, take a screwtop jar of home-made soup with you in the winter. You can heat it in a tin mug in the kettle.

Pizza

Dough:

275g (½ lb.) plain flour
1 teaspoonful salt
1 tablespoonful margarine
1 egg (can be left out)
1 teaspoonful sugar
2 teaspoonsful dried yeast
Almost 150ml (¼ pt.) water

Topping:

2 tablespoonsful oil
1 large onion
Medium-sized tin of tomatoes
2 tablespoonsful mixed herbs
Pepper and salt
Grated cheese

Warm the water, stir in the sugar, sprinkle yeast on top and leave to become frothy. Sieve salt and flour, rub in the margarine, add beaten egg and yeasty mixture. Knead, leave in a bowl to rise until double in size.

Fry the onions in oil until soft, stir in the tomatoes (not the liquid), add herbs and seasoning.

Knead the dough and flatten out into a baking tin (I use my paella dish). Spoon topping over, grate cheese on top and bake at gas mark 6, 400°F/200°C for half an hour. If you're dressing this up for a party, you can add anchovies and olives as decoration. If you have no tomatoes, use grated carrot instead, or half tomatoes and half carrot.

Quiche Lorraine

For the pastry:

175g (6 oz.) plain flour
Pinch of salt
75g (3 oz.) lard and margarine mixed

For the filling:

100g (4 oz.) scraps of bacon
1 medium onion/sliced leek or spring onions
2 eggs
150ml ($\frac{1}{4}$ pt.) top of the milk
Salt and pepper
50g (2 oz.) grated cheese

Make the pastry and roll out to fit an 8-inch sandwich tin, or flan ring (if you're so lucky).

Peel and chop the onion, cut the bacon pieces into strips and fry these gently together. There should be enough fat from the bacon. Place in flan case.

Beat up the eggs. Gradually beat in the milk, then add cheese, pepper and salt and pour into flan case.

Bake at gas mark 5, 375°F/190°C for 35 minutes or until filling is set.

Cornish Pasties, Spinach or Nettle-top Pasties

Make pastry with 100g (4 oz.) flour to 50g (2oz.) fat. Roll out and cut circles round a saucer, or a coffee cup saucer if you want dainty ones.

For Cornish Pasties, put a spoonful of potato and mince mixture (leftover Shepherd's Pie) in the centre, moisten the edges, draw up and pinch together.

Bake in a hot oven, gas mark 7, 425°F/220°C for 20 minutes, then reduce heat to gas mark 5, 375°F/190°C for a further 20 minutes.

Filling for Spinach or Nettle Pasties:

450g (1 lb) spinach or nettle tops
25g (1 oz.) margarine
Salt and pepper
Grated nutmeg
Ground ginger
1 egg
100g (4 oz.) grated cheese

If you are using nettle tops, wear rubber gloves. Wash the nettles and throw away the stalks. Put tops and leaves in large pan half-filled with boiling salted water and cook for 10 minutes or until tender. Cook spinach in the same way. Drain and chop roughly.

Melt butter in saucepan, toss nettles or spinach in it. Remove from heat and add salt, pepper, nutmeg and ginger. Beat eggs and add them and the cheese to the green mixture.

Chicken Filling:

450g (1 lb) cooked boned chicken
2 tablespoonsful margarine
2 tablespoonsful flour
275ml (½ pt.) hot chicken stock
Salt, pepper, nutmeg
1 egg

Make a sauce from the margarine, flour and stock, add seasoning, then beaten egg and chicken. Fill pasties as for Cornish.

Scotch Eggs

450g (1 lb) sausagemeat
5 hard-boiled eggs
1 beaten egg
Crisp breadcrumbs

Shell eggs. Divide sausagemeat into five pieces. Flatten each piece on a floured plate into a round big enough to cover the eggs. Wrap round the eggs, smoothing until there are no cracks. Brush with beaten egg and roll in breadcrumbs.

Heat fat in chip pan to a medium heat and lower eggs in the basket. Fry for about 5 minutes, then drain on paper. I use an opened paper bag for draining fatty food.

You can use the recipe for Oatmeal Sausages for the covering, which will make the sausagemeat go further.

Sausage Rolls

Make quick flaky pastry as follows:

225g ($\frac{1}{2}$ lb) plain flour
150g (6 oz.) margarine and lard mixed and frozen solid
Pinch of salt
A little water

Sieve flour and salt and grate the fat in flakes on a coarse grater. Mix in with knife and add water to a soft consistency. Leave in a cool place, while you prepare Oatmeal Sausage mixture. Roll out the pastry and cut into squares of whatever size you fancy for mini or ordinary sausage rolls. Put a piece of sausage mixture on each, roll up and fix with water. Bake at gas mark 7, 425°F/220°C for 20 minutes, then reduce heat to gas mark 5, 375°F/190°C for further 20 minutes.

Apple Turnover

Make pastry as for Cornish Pasties and fill with chopped apple and sultanas or jam and apple mixture.

Orange Mousse and Fresh Fruit Salad

You'll find the recipes in Chapter 9.

Jam Mould and Jam Jelly

Recipes in Chapter 6.

Packing Packed Lunches

Apart from saving the plastic boxes in which you buy ice-cream, also save small screwtop jars for puddings, cartons for salad, greaseproof paper from cereal packets, small plastic bags, and if you buy foil, wash it and use it again.

To avoid morning rush, you can pack the boxes the night before and keep everything fresh in the fridge. Sandwiches can be made in bulk and will keep fresh in the freezer for a month.

5

Good Hot Dinners

When our foremothers were cooking on the breadline, they served traditional British peasant food – thick vegetable soups with a hunk of home-made bread, stews where the meat went further because it was bulked out with vegetables and oatmeal. And they made suet crusts and pastry crusts for filling pies. They served Yorkshire pudding with gravy before the meal, to take the edge off the appetite for the precious meat course.

During the last war Lord Woolton told us what 'Food will win the War' and as we were still rationed for some time afterwards, we had to go on eating it. We did wonders with dried eggs, lentils, carrots and other vegetables, and the famous whale meat. I remember being sent to queue for it at the village fishmonger's, and we all agreed it was revolting. Some of the foods we were told to eat then have rocketted in price: for instance, spam and our ration of steak, which was then 1s.4d. a pound. Both are now in the treats class.

But today we are very, very lucky. Since this country has become so international, we can buy the basics for good peasant meals from many countries. Hard-up Italians have always made delicious pasta dishes. The Spanish, Indians and Chinese have done wonders with rice. And now we can have all the different types of beans (with as much protein in them as beef), sweet potatoes, green bananas and Chinese lettuce to mention but a few of the ingredients cooks on the breadline in other countries have always used to keep their families happy.

I haven't room here to re-hash Britain's staple dishes, so hope you'll look in your mother's or grandmother's cookery books for the many soups (are you still throwing away pea pods?), stews (made from forgotten parts of the animal), and all those lovely puddings which have gone out of fashion since we found a mousse in the supermarket, or yogurt with a couple of raspberries. When did you last cook Lemon Sponge, Spotted Dick and Jam Roly-Poly? And what about home-made rice pudding with that lovely brown skin, and baked egg custard and all the delicious summer desserts like Summer Pudding – made with blackberries straight from the bush, windfall apples and bread.

As I've usually been hard up, my children have learned to enjoy all types of food, and can twiddle up their spaghetti as quickly as any Umberto can in Sicily.

Here are some of our favourites:

Thick Onion Soup

Peel and slice about 450g (1 lb) onions, cook gently in a heavy pan with a little margarine until tender, but not brown. Keep the lid on the pan while you're doing this. Now add a couple of tablespoons of flour and stir into the onions. Cover with stock, or milk and water. Season with peppercorns and salt. You can thicken with left-over mashed potato or oatmeal instead of flour. Cook gently, stirring occasionally, until thick and creamy.

Fry up some small squares of bread. Put the soup in bowls and drop the croutons on top.

You can also make this soup with leeks. Use the green tops as well, sliced finely.

Stock (and Dripping)

Always boil up bones and carcases in a big pot and make your own stock. Allow to cool and skim off any fat, which you can use as it is when you start off a stew or soup, or to baste your joint. Clarified, you can use it for cakes. Ask the butcher for marrow bones – they produce a lovely lot of white fat. Do boil your stockpot up once a day.

Monday Soup

Look in the fridge and get out the weekend leftovers. If you have a small Yorkshire pud, a portion of chicken on rice, some mashed or roast potato and peas, remains of gravy, bread sauce, or even a slice of meat pie, don't throw them out. Mince all the solid objects up and add them to this basic recipe.

Peel and slice 450g (I lb) of onions and carrots and cook them in a little fat in a pan with the lid on for a few minutes, shaking from time to time to prevent sticking. Add all your leftovers, seasoning, a pinch of mixed herbs, stock (and a beef stock cube if you'd like it to look brown). Cover with stock or water. Cook until all is tender, thicken with oatmeal if too thin, and add some more seasoning if necessary. Mash it with a potato masher, or put through a sieve. You can add a handful of macaroni or pearl barley if you like.

This soup, served with bread, with fresh fruit to follow, is a nourishing, filling meal that is easy to prepare.

Twenty-one Ways With Mince

Use 225g ($\frac{1}{2}$ lb) onions (or more) to 1 lb mince, and add chopped carrot if you like. Cook this gently in a heavy pan with a little fat (very little, as the fat will come out of the mince), then add a tin of tomatoes if you have them, mixed herbs, seasoning, stock and a handful of oats to thicken. Simmer for about half an hour. If you add the oats at the last minute they will look like meat and take on the flavour of the sauce.

One weekend, when very broke and with six of us to feed, I served this with vegetables one lunchtime, and in lasagne on the Sunday. So 1 lb of mince made twelve helpings. Our little friend, Francesca, from the town houses down the road was not sure about the lasagne when it arrived on the table. 'We're having pork at home,' she said. 'I've never had meat with custard before.' But my kids urged her to try it, or could they have her helping? She ended up asking for the recipe to take home to her mother.

You can do a great deal with mince. It doesn't have to be boring. Here are some suggestions for serving.

1. With potatoes and green vegetables.
2. With a suet crust.

3. With a pastry crust.
4. Topped with mashed potato, as for Shepherd's Pie.
5. In Cornish Pasties (see page 34).
6. Serve basic recipe with spaghetti, macaroni or any fancy pasta.
7. In lasagne or canneloni.
8. Make it into beefburgers.
9. Mince loaf (follow recipe for sausage loaf on p. 46).
10. Add it to vegetable soup.
11. Service basic recipe on toast.
12. To fill mashed potato nests.
13. To stuff green peppers, served on rice.
14. To stuff large onions.
15. To stuff marrow.
16. In cabbage leaf parcels. Cook the leaves for 3 minutes, lay them in a dish, put mince in the middle, roll up and keep in parcels with a cocktail stick. Re-heat.
17. In baked potatoes.
18. In hotpot, with more vegetables.
19. In rolls.
20. Curried.
21. Mixed up with cooked parsnip and potato, and fried as patties.

Make Your Own Pasta

If Italian mama can do it, so can you. It's really very easy to make lasagne, cannelloni, ravioli, tagliatelle, and I also make animal shapes with biscuit cutters, which amuses the children. Animali and tomato sauce makes a change from spaghetti.

Basic Pasta Recipe

450g (1 lb) plain flour
1 teaspoonful salt
2 eggs
4-5 tablespoonsful water

Sift flour and salt into a large mixing bowl. Make a well in the centre and pour in the beaten eggs. Add 2 tablespoonsful water and mix together with your fingertips until it forms a ball, adding

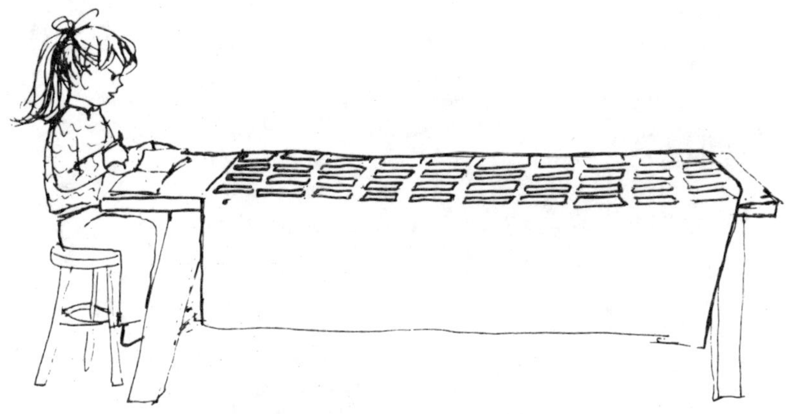

'Mum! Why can't you buy lasagne like normal people?'

more water as necessary.

Knead the dough on a floured working surface until it is smooth and elastic, sprinkling with a little more flour to stop it sticking to your hands. Knead for about 15 minutes, turning it over four times (I use the egg timer for guidance). If you find this boring, try singing.

Divide the dough into four equal parts and roll out one piece at a time until it is paper thin. Sprinkle with flour, fold over and roll out again. Repeat this twice more. Make sure it *is* paper thin, then cut into 2 x 10cm (2 x 4-inch) strips for lasagne, (3 x 4-inch) rectangles for cannelloni and 6mm ($\frac{1}{4}$-inch) strips for tagliatelle.

Leave to dry for an hour. You can hang the tagliatelle on the kitchen airer. I lay the lasagne on a piece of clean sheet on the living room table and anyone who wants to use the table grumbles. But I take no notice. You can use the pasta after an hour, but I usually leave it longer to dry completely, and pack it in tins. Cannelloni is dried for an hour before being used, and ravioli is dried after being made up into pockets.

Ravioli

Meat filling:

350g ($\frac{3}{4}$ lb) minced beef
2 tablespoonsful margarine
1 tablespoonful olive oil
2 tablespoonsful grated cheese
2 tablespoonsful dry breadcrumbs
1 tablespoonful chopped parsley
Nutmeg or cinnamon
Salt and black pepper

Gently fry the meat in margarine and olive oil. Leave to cool, then stir in the other ingredients.

Divide basic pasta dough in half. Roll out 3mm ($\frac{1}{8}$ inch) thick into two squares. Cut one of these into 5cm (2-inch) strips. Put teaspoons of the filling on the large square at 5cm (2-inch) intervals. Dip your finger in a cup of water and dampen pasta around the filling. Then place your 2-inch strips on top of the filling and press down well around the meat. I then use a little wooden wheel cutter to divide the ravioli into sachets with deckle edges. Leave the ravioli for 2 hours and then boil in salted water for about 15 minutes. Do not overcook pasta. It should be just biteable, not soggy. Serve with tomato sauce (your own).

Cannelloni

When the rectangles of dough have dried for an hour, drop them into boiling water for 5 minutes. Drop into cold water. Drain on cloth to dry. Fill with meat mixture, roll up and place in a greased ovenproof dish. Cover with cheese sauce. Bake for 30 minutes at gas mark 3, 325°F/170°C.

You can make the filling more interesting by adding chopped mushrooms or onion.

Cheese Sauce

This is a basic cheese sauce to use with lasagne, cannelloni, cauliflower cheese, macaroni cheese. Ever tried leeks in cheese sauce?

2 tablespoonsful margarine
2 tablespoonsful flour

½l (1 pt.) milk, or milk and water
4 tablespoonsful grated cheese
Salt and black pepper

Melt the margarine in a pan, remove from heat and stir in the flour. Mix in a little hot water or milk and stir well over the heat, then gradually add the rest of the liquid. Cook gently until it thickens. Season to taste. This keeps very well in a screwtop jar in the fridge for a week.

Tomato Sauce

I make enough of this to use with the pasta and also to serve with anything the family would otherwise plaster with bought sauce.

1 small onion
2 tablespoonsful margarine
A little cooking oil
400g (14 oz.) tin of tomatoes
1 dessertspoonful brown sugar
Clove of garlic (optional)
Finely chopped parsley
Salt and pepper

Fry the very finely chopped onion and crushed garlic gently in the oil and margarine. Add the other ingredients and simmer for 10 minutes. Put through a sieve. Thicken as desired with cornflour.

Keep the surplus in a screwtop jar in the fridge and serve in a small dish with a teaspoon with things like beefburgers and sausages.

Spaghetti

I discovered that a friend of ours had never cooked spaghetti because he thought it needed an enormous rectangular pan. He was very sad about it, and very excited when I told him he did not need an enormous rectangular pan.

If that's what putting you off, I'd better tell you how to go about it!

Boil a large, ordinary pan of salted water, hold your bundle of spaghetti and put one end into the water. As it softens it will curl round in the pan until you have the whole lot under water.

Serve with mince mixture (basic recipe p. 39), with grated

cheese on top if you're feeling extravagant.

Allow 50g (2 oz.) pasta for a small child, 75g (3 oz.) or 100g (4 oz.) for bigger children and adults. I usually yell from the kitchen: 'Are you 3 or 4 ounce people today?'

If any is left over, you can always chop it up and add it to your next pot of soup just before serving.

My Macaroni

I chop up some onions, put them in a big pan and cook for 5 minutes, then add long macaroni, broken up into 10cm (4-inch) pieces). Snap them over the pan, or you get the floor littered with funny little triangular pieces which fly away as you snap.

Make a cheese sauce (p. 42) while the macaroni is cooking. Drain the macaroni and onions. Put into an ovenproof dish, stir some tinned tomatoes into it, and the cheese sauce. Heat through.

Lasagne

Cook lasagne in boiling water for 8 minutes. Drain. Fill ovenproof dish with lasagne and mince layers. Top with cheese sauce. Heat through.

Rice Dishes

A Malayan student lodger showed me how to cook rice perfectly, without the bore of running it under the tap after cooking.

Measure it by the cupful into a sieve and rinse under the cold tap to get rid of starch. Put into a pan with 2 cups of water to each cup of rice. Add salt, and the secret ingredient – a knob of butter. Bring to the boil, give it a stir, put the lid on firmly and leave it to simmer very, very gently until the rice is cooked and the liquid absorbed. This should take about 15 minutes. Give it an occasional stir to prevent sticking. If any does stick to the bottom of the pan, and is not burnt, just cover with water and leave for a while. You can spoon it out easily and add to next pot of soup.

Serve chicken and/or mushrooms in a white sauce on rice.

Or curry anything you have – vegetables, leftovers of meat. For a treat top with slices of hard-boiled egg.

A deliciously refreshing accompaniment for curry – crush a clove of garlic, mix with plain yogurt, stir in slices of cucumber and sprinkle with cayenne.

Basic Curry Recipe

An Indian student lodger told me that real curry should be cooked for at least 8 hours, but you can compromise by cooking it one day, leaving it overnight for the flavours to infuse, and then re-heating.

Fry up some onions and a tablespoon of curry powder in a little oil, then add sultanas, nuts (I sometimes use a packet of nuts and raisins), a little grated lemon peel, chopped apple and your other ingredients – pieces of meat or chicken and vegetables. Cook very gently for at least half an hour. Thicken with cornflour. Vary the amount of curry powder according to how hot your family likes it. Small children do not like hot curry, but can be gradually introduced to it by hotting it up slightly as the years go by. If they really loathe it, cook some of the vegetables and meat for them in a white sauce, and the rest with curry powder for the adults.

Lentil Roast Duck

This is a very economical meal when you're really broke.

Leave 225g (8 oz.) lentils to soak overnight and then cook them in their own water, with a large chopped onion, until tender. Add more water as they swell and absorb it. Boil 450g (1 lb) potatoes. Mash potatoes and lentil mixture together, add 225g (8 oz.) breadcrumbs and season well.

If you were good at plasticine when you were a child, you can now shape the mixture into a duck, complete with legs, and place on a baking tin. Baste with fat as you would a real joint, and cook in the oven for 1½ hours, basting occasionally.

You can keep back some of the mixture to make patties to serve at another meal with salad or vegetables.

If you have a real chicken, you could carve one side for one meal, plaster the bare side with lentil roast mixture, re-cook and serve what looks like a complete bird, carving alternate slices from each side.

My family were most suspicious when I first produced Lentil Roast Duck, but we have it regularly now. Only problem is, there's no carcas afterwards to make soup.

Sausage Loaf

One of my sister Edwina's favourite creations. It makes sausagemeat spread a lot further.

2 tomatoes
450g (1 lb) sausagemeat
1 small onion, chopped
2 apples
75g (3 oz.) breadcrumbs or oats
1 egg

Fry the onion and chopped apples with the sausagemeat. You shouldn't need any fat as it will come out of the sausagemeat. Arrange tomato slices in the base of a rectangular tin, then add the rest of the ingredients mixed up together and bound with the egg.

Bake for 45 minutes at gas mark 5, 375°F/190°C.

Turn out on to a dish and garnish with thin slices of apple. Serve hot with vegetables, or cold with salad.

You will find other favourite family dishes in the section on entertaining, and more kids' stuff in the next chapter.

6

Kids' Stuff

'I'm hungry, Mum.'

It's the recurring cry of your children from birth until they go out into the big world to forage for their own food. So how are you going to feed them on your ever-tightening budget?

Again, don't buy it – make it. All the things that children love to eat can be made at home – from baby food to baked beans, fish fingers, yogurt, crisps and ice-cream.

Feeding the Baby

Babies can be expensive little creatures and we were very broke when our first was born. So she had a second-hand cot and pram, home-made clothes, blankets, cot sheets and nappies saved from my younger brother's trousseau. And I fed her myself. I ate normally, but drank pints and pints of water, and hey presto – the baby was naturally provided for.

I noticed as I produced the next five children over the years that fashions in feeding changed; when I had the sixth a nurse appeared with some pills and when I asked what they were for, she said: 'To dry up your milk, dear.' I said I was planning to feed the baby myself and she said disapprovingly: 'No one else is in *my* ward.' I was worried she might spike my morning tea! Apparently it upset the ward routine, and caused 'unrest' among the other mums who had to wait for the tray of bottles. And I was not popular when I wandered distractedly into the nursery at 2 a.m. demanding my child. 'Go back to bed, Mother. We'll be giving him some boiled water.' So I cried, snatched up my child like a lady from the jungle and said: 'But I've *got* to feed him. Or I'll burst.'

There is a swing back to natural feeding these days. The experts have come up with the idea that human milk is okay for human babies after all. And cow's milk is really for calves. But for heaven's sake don't feel guilty if you can't make it and have to buy it. The hospital, clinic or health visitor will guide you safely to the right stuff for the little darling.

But one really wonderful thing about feeding the baby yourself is that you know the milk is the right consistency, the right temperature, sterilized and can't upset him – unless you've been eating something really acid, or have been to a wedding reception. My first baby was awfully sleepy for days after we had been to a champagne reception. She just dozed with a happy smile on her face and seemed to burp more than usual.

It never occurred to me to buy tinned food. I bought baby cereal, clinic orange juice and vitamins to begin with and by the time the baby was five months old she was having a few spoonsful of family meals, suitably *puréed*, and later mashed.

Suitable or Unsuitable?

As I had helped to look after my younger brothers and sisters, I automatically knew that babies should not have: fried food or fatty food; lumpy things, or they choked; sour or acid fruit; gristly meat; cups of tea; salt or too much sugar; spicy things; and I knew they definitely needed, just as we did: at least a pint of milk a day; something filling – cereal, potato; green vegetables; fruit; orange juice; the clinic's dose of vitamins; and they liked gravy, egg yolk, cheese, and rusks to chew, but you had to watch them.

If your family are eating a balanced diet, most of it will be suitable, and you can sieve the baby's portion of it for the first few months, and then mash it so that it is a little lumpier when he gets a few teeth.

New and inexperienced mums can obtain a great deal of gentle advice on feeding their babies when they take them to the baby clinic to be weighed or checked or innoculated or whatever.

My mother never left any of her babies with a bottle propped up on a pillow, because, apart from the danger of choking, she said the cuddle was as important as the bottle, and we older children took turns to feed the baby, burp it and get it off to sleep. I used to sit on a grassy bank with my homework and a string tied to my ankle, letting the pram roll slowly back and then pulling it towards me, while the baby watched the leaves and sky and cooed off to sleep. The burping was most important, or the baby cried and had to be got up and re-burped.

When the baby starts to take more solid food at about four or five months old, remember he is conservative and can object to new tastes. Go carefully if you don't want to be spat at. Introduce one new taste at a time. Let him get used to it, and then try another. If your baby really doesn't like something, leave it off the menu. It seems ironic but poor little babies have been forced to eat puréed spinach for years (most of them objecting strongly) and now its nutritional value has been found to be not all that exceptional. Put yourself in the baby's place. Would you like to be strapped in a chair, wearing a sweaty plastic bib and have a spoon of bitter green stuff descending relentlessly. I'm sure you'd scream and spit. I was a very clever baby. I used to put my plate of dinner upside down on my head if I didn't like it.

I was a very clever baby.

Don't force your baby to eat everything you've prepared, just because it's there. Remember you have days when you don't feel all that hungry. He does too. And although I do try to stress 'waste not, want not', don't eat up his leftovers. It will ruin your figure.

Family Menus

Here are some family menus and suggestions for feeding the baby:

1. Liver casserole, potatoes, marrow
   Apple pie and custard
   (Baby gets mashed potato and marrow, gravy from the casserole. Apple from the pie, mashed and mixed with custard.)
2. Sunday joint, Yorkshire pud, potatoes, peas
   Orange mousse
   (Baby gets boiled potatoes, peas and gravy mashed up. A little mousse.)
3. Fish and potato pie, green beans
   Rhubarb crumble and custard
   (Baby gets fish pie (searched again for bones) and mashed up beans. *Spot* of rhubarb, custard.
4. Soup, Pizza and salad
   Fresh fruit
   (Baby gets fish pie – searched for bones – and mashed up beans. *Spot* of rhubarb, custard).
5. Cheese soufflé, potatoes, spinach
   Fresh fruit salad
   (Baby gets all of first course, mashed or sieved. Soft fruits from fruit salad.)

Always remember to keep the baby's utensils and your sieve really clean. Sterilize them with boiling water.

At about six months, babies like chewing things, and you can make your own rusks. This is useful, particularly as so many older children raid the baby's rusk tin – which can be expensive if you buy them.

Rusks

Take some 1 cm ($\frac{1}{2}$-inch) thick slices of bread, cut into fingers and put on a baking tray. Bake at gas mark 1, 275°F/140°C for about 30 minutes, turning them over halfway through. They should be light brown.

Children's Favourites

Baked Beans

Make them for half the price. Soak haricot beans overnight in cold water. Add more water and simmer slowly until soft. This can take two hours, so I usually put mine in a casserole with the lid on, at the bottom of the oven while something else is cooking. When cooked, mix in your own tomato sauce (page 43).

Pork and Beans

Mix beans with cubes of salt pork, seasoning, a little mustard, 2 tablespoonsful treacle, your own tomato sauce and two sliced onions. Cook slowly for 4 hours.

Beefburgers

450g (1 lb) raw mince
50g (2 oz.) breadcrumbs or oats
1 egg
3 tablespoonsful milk
Salt and pepper

Put the minced beef into a bowl, break it up with a fork and stir in breadcrumbs (or oats), egg and milk. Add seasoning. Divide into 6 to 8 rounds, 1cm (½ inch) thick on a floured plate. Fry as usual.

Sausages and Sausage Rolls

Recipes on pages 31 and 36.

Fish Fingers

Buy white fish, skin it and cut it into strips. Roll in egg and breadcrumbs, or coat with a flour and water batter.

Cheese Soufflé

2 eggs
25g (1 oz.) margarine
12g (½ oz.) flour

150ml ($\frac{1}{4}$ pt.) milk
75g (3 oz.) grated cheese

Separate eggs. melt margarine and stir in flour. Add milk gradually and bring mixture to the boil. Cool a little. Add beaten yolks and grated cheese. Whisk egg whites stiffly and fold in. Pour into a well-greased dish. You can use a soufflé dish, making a paper collar so that the soufflé rises out of the dish, but if you're in a hurry there's no reason why you shouldn't just cook it in an ordinary dish.

Bake at gas mark 6, 400°F/200°C for half an hour until well risen and brown. Serve at once or it will collapse.

Cheese Crockets

6 tablespoonsful mashed potato
4 tablespoonsful grated cheese
4 tablespoonsful milk
2 tablespoonsful crushed cornflakes
Egg yolk
Pepper and salt

Mix egg, cheese, mashed potato and seasoning. Make into patties. Roll in cornflake crumbs. Bake on a greased tin at gas mark 4, 350°F/180°C for 30 minutes.

You can make these with mashed swede, carrot or turnip instead of potato.

Colcannon

Use the same quantities of cold boiled potatoes and cabbage. Mash up potatoes and cabbage. Season and mix in 25g (1 oz.) margarine or dripping to each pound of mixture. Put into a dish, make an artistic pattern on top and heat through in the oven until brown on top. You could decorate it with sliced tomatoes and bacon scraps.

Creamy Fish Pie

Use any white fish for this, and the same weight in potatoes. Cook the potatoes and mash them. Cook the fish and remove bones and skin. Make a white sauce, mix the fish into it and put it in an ovenproof dish. Squeeze lemon juice over it. Top with the mashed potato and heat through in the oven. Decorate with parsley sprigs. If you like, you can put chopped parsley in the sauce.

Lemon Pudding

1 cupful stale bread
1 cupful water
2 tablespoonsful sugar
1 tablespoonful shredded suet
1 egg yolk
Juice and rind of a lemon

Soak the bread in the water, then beat it to a pulp. Add sugar, suet, egg yolk, and lemon. Bake until set. You can top it with meringue if you like, or serve with lemon sauce.

Velvet Pudding

Make a pint of custard, using half milk, half water. When cool, but not set, fold in one or two whisked egg whites.

First Forgotten Pudding

Yorkshire pudding, reheated and served spread with jam and 'drowned' in custard. Make twice as many individual Yorkshire puds as you need for lunch, and serve the spare ones next day, scooping out the top and putting the jam inside.

Jam Mould

Melt 3 tablespoonsful jam or jelly in 3 teacups water. Mix up 1½ tablespoonsful cornflour with a little water and then mix altogether and boil until it thickens. Pour into wetted mould to set. You can also make this using fruit juice.

Jam Jelly

Boil ½l (1 pt.) water with 224g (½ lb) jam and 1 dessertspoonful sugar. Mix 25g (1 oz.) gelatine with a little water, add and boil for a minute. Pour through sieve into wetted mould.

Pixie's Jelly

Make a jelly with apple *purée* and gelatine. Add a spot of green colouring. Allow to set in a dish, then fork up the top a little. Stand pieces of banana in it for mushroom stalks and top with meringues. Make tiny toadstools with half glacé cherries, dotted with icing spots.

Mock Cream

Very useful to decorate your desserts or fill cakes:

50g (2 oz.) butter
50g (2 oz.) caster sugar
2 tablespoonsful boiling water
2 tablespoonsful top of the milk
Vanilla essence

Cream fat and sugar until soft and light. Beat in 2 tablespoonsful boiling water gradually. Add milk in same way. Flavour with vanilla.

Make Your Own Yogurt

If you are lucky enough to get hold of some yogurt plant (which looks like rice pudding), you can make endless supplies of yogurt simply by covering it with milk and leaving it in a warm place. However, this is not easy to come by, and you can make yogurt as follows:

Pour ½l (1 pt.) long-life milk into a saucepan and heat until it is warm to the finger. Transfer to a plastic box with a close fitting lid. Add 2 teaspoonsful of ordinary plain yogurt (bought from the shop) and mix well. Put the lid on the box tightly, wrap it in a towel and leave in a warm place until set. This will take from 12 to 24 hours.

The yogurt will now be ready to eat as it is, or you can add brown sugar or fruit. Put aside a few teaspoons to start the next batch. So you have an endless supply, and you can keep the set yogurt cool in the fridge.

Snacks

'I'm still hungry, Mum.'

Kids have become used to bags of crisps and other snacks, and to sweets and chocolates – while we never had it so good.

During the War you had a job finding sweets, and I can remember the great day when everyone received sweet ration coupons, entitling each one of us to 2 ounces of sweets a week. We got used to it, and didn't yearn for them. And I know my parents never bought us drinks like fizzy raspberry or coke. If we were thirsty, there was plenty of water in the tap. And I'm sure it was better for our stomachs.

I used to buy orange and lemon squash for my children, but it is so expensive now that it has just become a weekend treat, and I make our crisps and potato sticks. We also make toffee and fudge occasionally, and sometimes our own ice-cream.

Crisps

Peel a large potato, and slice it very, very finely. Dry with a cloth, fry in your chip pan, and drain well on paper.

Potato Sticks

Cut potato into very tiny chips and fry as above.

Treacle Toffee

450g (1 lb) brown sugar
50g (2 oz.) margarine
150ml (¼ pt.) water
100g (4 oz.) black treacle
100g (4 oz.) golden syrup.
A pinch of cream of tartar

Dissolve the sugar in the water, add the other ingredients and boil. Do not stir more than necessary. It makes things simpler if you have a thermometer as the syrup should reach the temperature of 260°F/135°C. However, I seem to manage without, and test the toffee for setting in a cup of cold water. Pour the toffee into a well-greased tin. When firm enough, mark it into squares. Remove from tin when cold.

Vanilla Fudge

275 ml (½ pt.) evaporated milk
450g (1 lb) sugar
37g (1½ oz.) margarine
Vanilla essence

Put milk, sugar and margarine into a strong pan and heat until sugar dissolves. Bring to the boil (to 238°F/120°C) stirring all the time. Then beat thoroughly as it thickens, pour into a greased tin, and cut into squares when firm.

Add the vanilla – or any other flavouring you like – as you beat the mixture.

Sugar Mice and Peppermint Creams

50g (2 oz.) powdered glucose
2 tablespoonsful boiling water
1 small egg white
About 450g (1 lb) sifted icing sugar

Pour the water on to the glucose. Beat the egg white a little. Mix together with the icing sugar. Knead. Make into mouse shapes, using white string for tails.

Use this same recipe with the addition of a few drops of peppermint essence and some green colouring if you want to make peppermint creams. Cut them into rounds with a small glass or cutter.

Leave to dry and become firm.

Chocolate Ice Cream

1 tablespoonful cocoa
1 tablespoonful custard powder
275ml (½ pt.) milk
50g (2 oz.) sugar
25g (1 oz.) margarine
150ml (¼ pt.) top of the milk

Mix custard powder and cocoa with a little milk, add sugar and the rest of the milk and bring to the boil. Remove from heat, add margarine, pour into a bowl and stir in the top of the milk. Whisk well. Put in freezer section of fridge. When frozen at the edges, whisk again and then freeze to an ice-cream consistency.

Water Ices

2 teaspoonsful gelatine
1 tablespoonful water
275ml (½ pt.) fruit juce
1 egg white

Dissolve the gelatine in water. Add the fruit juice. Freeze, stirring every quarter of an hour, until it looks like slush. Fold in the stiffly beaten egg white, return to the fridge and freeze.

It is very useful to be able to make your own ices and if you get a set of iced-lolly dishes you'll save a lot of money. The children will become quite interested in making their own simply by freezing orange squash. We don't have lolly dishes, and my children make them in some old plastic cups, using old lolly sticks. Don't let them use straight sided cups because the plastic cracks as the ice expands.

7

Bread, Cakes and Biscuits

I only go to the baker to buy large bags of flour, and fresh yeast (which is cheaper than dried). There are many advantages to making your own bread. You can laugh when a bread strike is threatened and everyone else is queueing and neurotically stocking up. And if you have extra visitors over a bank holiday and it looks as if you're running out, you can always make some more. You'll spend half the amount of money you would have spent on ready-made bread, and the house will be filled with a beautiful smell. And the end result is good, wholesome bread – not soggy cotton wool.

It isn't difficult to make, and although you have to wait for the dough to rise, you can be doing some other cooking during that time, or sitting somewhere with your feet up. I find the initial mixing takes me 10 to 15 minutes then I leave the dough to rise for 1 hour. After another 10 minutes of kneading I put it into tins and leave to 'prove' (that means to rise again) for 15 minutes and the baking takes just under an hour. But don't feel tied by the rising time. I've even forgotten the stuff overnight and baked it next morning. No problems.

I wouldn't dream of buying bread nowadays, and here are my basic family recipes. I bake once a week, and keep it fresh in the fridge in a polythene bag, or in the freezer. If it has been in the freezer, leave it overnight to thaw out. No need to bake again, but you can pop it in the oven if you wish.

Family Loaf (this makes 4 450g (1 lb) loaves)
1150g (2½ lb) plain flour
450g (1 lb) wholemeal flour
37g (1½ oz.) salt
50g (2 oz.) margarine
25g (1 oz.) yeast
1 teaspoonful sugar
1l (1¾ pt.) water (approx.)

Mix the flour and salt, rub in the fat with your fingers. Mix the yeast and sugar together with a teaspoon in a cup. This will make a creamy liquid. Add some of the water (warmed to blood heat). Mix well. Add the yeast mixture to the dry ingredients and mix in the remaining water. Knead it in the bowl for a few minutes, adding a sprinkling of flour and putting flour on your hands if it is very sticky. Cover with a cloth and leave in a warm place to rise for about an hour. It should double in size.

Knead the dough on a floured working surface for about 10 minutes until it is smooth and elastic. Half fill the greased loaf tins. Leave in a warm place for a further 10 minutes, then bake in a hot oven, gas mark 8, 450°F/230°C, for 15 minutes. Lower the temperature to gas mark 5, 375°F/190°C, and bake for a further half an hour to 40 minutes. When ready the bread should be slightly brown on top, well risen, and it should sound hollow when you rap it underneath with your knuckles. Put it on a wire rack to cool.

If you do burn it, you can use a fine grater to get rid of the black!

If you use dried yeast, put some of the tepid water in a pan with the sugar, sprinkle the yeast on top and leave to become frothy before adding to the dry ingredients.

Rolls
You can use the Family Loaf recipe to make rolls, or use all plain flour instead of the mixture of plain and wholemeal. Shape the dough into rolls and bake for about 15 minutes on a greased baking tray.

Currant Milk Loaf

675g (1½ lb) plain flour
½ teaspoonful salt
50g (2 oz.) margarine
1 teaspoonful caster sugar
275ml (½ pt.) tepid milk
12g (½ oz.) yeast
75g (3 oz.) currants

Proceed as for Family Loaf, adding the currants to the dry ingredients before mixing in the milk and yeast mixture.

French Bread

Of course you won't be able to make those long, long, long loaves that Paris workmen cycle about with, but you're bound to influence friends and win people!

675g (1½ lb) plain flour
1 tablespoonful salt
1 tablespoonful butter or margarine
1 teaspoonful sugar
1 level tablespoonful yeast
275ml (½ pt.) tepid water
Sprinkling of yellow cornmeal

(This is to sprinkle on the greased baking sheet; it gives a crisp undercrust and makes sure you get a dusting of it on yourself and all over the kitchen, just as if you'd bought it from a genuine French bakery.)

Mix the dough as for Family Loaf, leave to rise for an hour, then punch it down ruthlessly, and leave to rise for another hour. Knead very well before dividing the dough into three. Roll each piece out to measure approximately 35cm (14 inches) by 20cm (8 inches). This isn't easy. It will keep springing back, but talk and roll it into submission. Taking the long side, roll each piece into a long sausage, place on the baking tray and make four crosswise slashes on the top. Put a dish of water in the oven. Bake at gas mark 6, 400°F/200°C, for 50 minutes, brushing the top with water twice during the process. This will make it crisp and shiny.

Malt Loaf

450g (1 lb) self-raising flour

2 level teaspoonsful bicarbonate of soda
4 tablespoonsful black treacle
4 tablespoonsful malt extract
275ml (½ pt.) milk and water
2 eggs
2 teacupsful sultanas or raisins

Sift flour and bicarbonate of soda. Melt treacle and malt in the milk. Add beaten eggs. Pour this mixture into the flour. Mix. Add fruit. Pour into a greased tin. Bake at gas mark 6, 400°F/200°C, for 15 minutes. Lower heat to gas mark 5, 375°F/190°C, for a further half-hour. Makes a lovely moist, gooey loaf.

Use a child (with clean hands) to help when kneading bread. They enjoy it. One of mine gets rid of a lot of aggro that way.

Hot Cross Buns (makes 12)
350g (12 oz.) plain flour
Pinch of salt
1 teaspoonful mixed spice
½ teaspoonful ground cinnamon
½ teaspoonful ground cloves
50g (2oz.)margarine
75g (3 oz.) caster sugar
100g (4 oz.) dried fruit
25g (1 oz.) chopped candied peel
25g (1 oz.) fresh or dried yeast
150ml (¼ pt.) milk and water (approx.)
1 egg
To glaze:
1 tablespoonful sugar mixed with 1 tablespoonful hot water

Sieve flour, salt and spices. Rub in the fat. Add the sugar, keeping back 1 teaspoonful. Add the fruit and peel. Cream the yeast and sugar, add the milk to it, and tip all into the flour mixture. Mix and knead the dough. Leave to prove for 1 to 2 hours, until it doubles in size. Divide into 12 balls. Make crosses by piping a firm flour and water mixture on the top. Leave to prove for 20 minutes. Bake at gas mark 7, 425°F/220°C, for 12 minutes. Brush the cooked buns with the sugar and water mixture.

Cakes

If you can make a Victoria cake and an ordinary nursery sponge there are dozens of ways in which you can use them: by adding flavouring – grated lemon peel to the dry mixture, and the juice of the lemon to the filling; by adding cocoa or coffee, and leaving out the same amount of flour; by decorating them with buttercream or icing (any colour), plus small sweets or your own icing sugar flowers. Victoria cake can be used as a topping for fruit puddings and in the creation of Upside Down Apple Cake. The sponge can be sandwiched with strawberries and cream or used as the basis of a fruit flan, setting the fruit with gelatine before putting it on top.

Victoria Cake or Fairy Cakes

(Makes 12 small cakes, or 1 sandwich cake)

100g (4 oz.) self-raising flour
50g (2 oz.) margarine
50g (2 oz.) caster sugar
1 egg
2 tablespoonsful milk

Cream the sugar and margarine together. Beat the eggs, then stir into the creamed mixture. Fold in some of the flour. Add milk alternately with the rest of the flour. Grease two sandwich tins and divide the mixture between them, or half fill 12 paper cases. Bake towards the top of the oven at gas mark 6, 400°F/200°C.

The sandwich cake will take about 20 minutes, and the fairy cakes about 15. Test them with a skewer. If it comes away clean, the cakes are ready. Turn on to a wire tray to cool.

This is a good starter recipe for children. Mine like making it in the tiny paper cases used for sweets – suitable for dolls' tea parties. And they enjoy decorating them.

Sponge Cake

Sponge cakes do take a few eggs, but they are perfect for small children, because they are light and easy to digest.

4 eggs
175g (6 oz.) caster sugar
100g (4 oz.) plain flour

Whisk the eggs and sugar in a bowl over a pan of hot water until thick. Sift in the flour, then fold it lightly into the egg mixture. Pour into 17cm (7 inch) cake tin, greased and dusted with sugar and flour. Bake in a moderate oven, gas mark 4, 350°F/180°C, for about an hour.

Slice across and sandwich together with jam.

Stale sponge and Victoria cake can be used for trifles. You can keep it in a screwtop jar in the fridge until needed.

Eggless Chocolate Cake

I am going into cups. 'What is a cup?' you may ask. Well, I mean an aunty's tea cup, not Dad's breakfast mug.

50g (2 oz.) plain chocolate
1 teacupful milk
75g (3 oz.) margarine
1¾ cupsful self-raising flour
¾ teaspoonful bicarbonate of soda
Pinch of salt
1 teacupful sugar
1 teaspoonful vanilla essence.

Melt the chocolate and margarine in the milk in a bowl over a pan of boiling water. Beat well and allow to cool a little. Sift the flour, salt and soda together in a bowl and stir in the sugar. Add the vanilla to the chocolate mixture and gradually stir in the dry ingredients, beating well. Divide between two very well greased sandwich tins and bake for about 20 minutes at gas mark 4, 350°F/180°C. Put together with buttercream filling.

My family love this cake filled with ice-cream, and eat it 'all posh' with a fork.

Tanner's Apple Cake

This is a delicious, moist cake, which you can serve hot or cold, and as a pudding if you like. The recipe has been passed down through our family for years, and is a good way of using up windfall apples.

225g (8 oz.) self-raising flour
100g (4 oz.) sugar
50g (2 oz.) currants
225g (8 oz.) chopped apple

100g (4 oz.) margarine
Milk to mix

Crumble the margarine and flour, stir in the currants, apple and sugar, and mix to a sticky consistency with milk. Turn into a greased loaf tin. Bake for 10 minutes at gas mark 6, 400°F/200°C. Reduce to gas mark 4, 350°F/180°C, and cook for about three-quarters of an hour, until brown on top.

Dripping Cake

225g (½ lb) self-raising flour
Pinch of salt
½ teaspoonful mixed spice
¼ teaspoonful ginger
75g (3 oz.) demerara sugar
75g (3 oz.) clarified dripping
50g (2 oz.) candied peel
75g (3 oz.) mixed dried fruit
1 egg
Milk to mix

Rub dripping into the flour, salt and spices. Stir in the sugar, dried fruit and candied peel. Beat in the egg and enough milk to make a dropping consistency. Turn into a well greased tin and bake for an hour at gas mark 4, 350°F/180°C.

1916 Trench Cake

225g (½ lb) flour
75g (3 oz.) cleaned currants
1 teaspoonful vinegar
150ml (¼ pt.) milk
75g (3 oz.) brown sugar
100g (4 oz.) margarine
2 teaspoonsful cocoa
½ teaspoonful baking soda
Nutmeg, ginger, grated lemon rind

Rub the margarine into the flour. Add the dry ingredients and mix well. Add the soda, dissolved in the vinegar and milk. Beat well. Turn into a greased cake tin. Bake at gas mark 4, 350°F/180°C, for 2 hours. Of course, if you're doing this in a trench, put a biscuit tin on bricks and keep the fire going underneath.

Our other family staples for the weekly bake-up are gingerbread and flapjack.

Biscuits

I was very worried about a student who was living on baked beans, so I gave him some elementary cooking lessons, and after that could not keep him out of the kitchen. He used to make the following biscuits almost by the hundredweight, and we have become quite hooked on them. (I'm back to cups again.)

Digestive Biscuits

100g (4 oz.) lard
2 cupsful flour
1 cupful sugar
1 teaspoonful baking powder
1 cupful oatmeal
Milk to mix

Rub the lard into the dry ingredients. Mix with milk to a soft dough. Roll out as thin as possible. Cut into small rounds and bake on a greased baking tray at gas mark 7, 425°F/220°C, until crisp: about 10 minutes.

You can ice them with melted chocolate if you like, and you then have chocolate digestive biscuits.

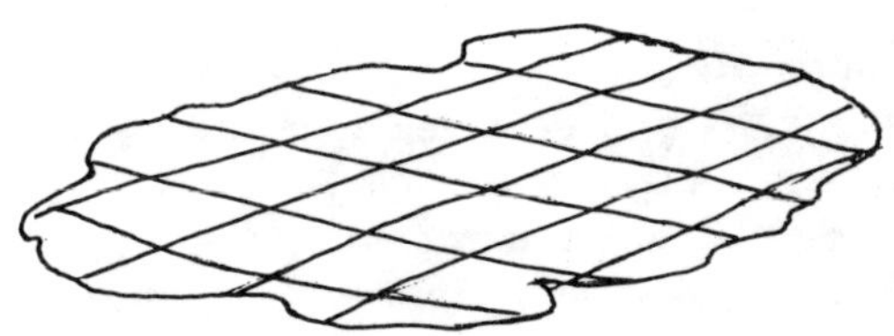

The quick way to cut out biscuits.

Carrot Cookies

225g (½ lb) raw carrots
75g (3 oz.) sugar
50g (2 oz.) margarine
75g (3 oz.) flour

Cream the margarine and nearly all the sugar together, keeping back one dessertspoonful. Grate the carrot and beat into the margarine and sugar. Fold in the flour. A tablespoonful of water can be added if the mixture seems dry. Drop spoonsful of the mixture on to a greased baking sheet. Sprinkle with sugar and cook at gas mark 7, 425°F/220°C, for 25 minutes. Eat hot or cold.

Ginger Crispies

3½ cupsful flour
1 teaspoonful salt
¾ tablespoonsful ground ginger
¼ tablespoonful ground mace
1 cupful golden syrup
½ cupful butter or margarine
¼ tablespoonful ground cinnamon
½ teaspoonful baking soda

Put the fat in a basin and stir in the warmed syrup. Mix in the dry ingredients. Leave to cool. Knead and roll out thinly. Cut into rounds with cutter or glass dipped in flour. Bake at gas mark 7. 425°F/220°C, for 5 minutes. Cool on a cake rack. This makes about 50 biscuits.

Filling and Decorating

Cake decorations are expensive, so use tiny sweets, grated chocolate, or pipe tiny coloured icing shapes on to greaseproof paper, and leave them to go hard before using.

The simplest icing is icing sugar mixed with water, but if you want a soft icing, use an egg white. You can flavour your icing with lemon juice, vanilla essence, black coffee, or a small amount of cocoa. Experiment until you find out the taste that suits you.

To me, that's what cookery is all about. Take a basic recipe, and then do your own thing – to make it your own creation.

8

How to Be a Squirrel

Once upon a time there was a caveman, and he hung a piece of meat up in his cave and it got all dried up by the smoke from the fire. And he found it didn't go bad, so he had something to chew in the long winter months when the blizzards were blowing and the animals were hiding.

There have always been ways of saving the gluts of summer and autumn to provide food in the cold, dark days. Our grandmothers went in for laying down beans in tubs of salt, and they strung up rings of apple and ran string through mushrooms to dry them. They preserved eggs in buckets of Waterglass. Meanwhile, grandfather had protected surplus root vegetables in a mound of straw, covered with earth. Before that the peasants hung meat and fish in their chimneys. And so the first kipper and the first ham were born.

Salting and bottling are not on my list of clever things to do. I did try bottling once, but it seemed a lot of bother, and you do have to have special jars, which are expensive – unless you find them in a jumble sale.

However, I am very glad I saved up for a small deep freeze, because this seems to me the easiest way of preserving food when it is plentiful. But is it so modern? The eskimos did it, and I remember reading about a Canadian family who shot a goose in October and hung it on a tree behind the house, so it froze solid – to be eaten on Christmas day.

I find pickling and chutneying foolproof. The vinegar and spices do the trick, and I've never had a failure. Jam making, too, is simple. And I've had some very good batches of wine, tasting finer than the cheap plonk you'd have to buy for entertaining otherwise.

Here are some of our favourite family recipes.

Pickles and Chutney

Don't use metal utensils for pickling, and save all your plastic screwtop jars to store the finished product. Metal lids go rusty. Make your own labels, or employ an artistic child. It is cheaper to cut up the large sticky labels used for re-cycling envelopes than to buy fancy ones. You can do pretty lettering and patterns with felt-tips. Another idea is to cut pictures of the fruit or vegetable from a gardening catalogue.

Pickled Onions

900g (2 lb) small onions
2 cupsful sugar
1 cupful salt
2 litres (2 quarts) vinegar
¼ cupful mixed allspice, cloves and peppercorns

Onions don't have to make you cry.

Peel the onions underwater (enlisting the help of anyone in the family who is mad about pickled onions. I have a son who wears swimming goggles while he does this, to stop his eyes watering.) Put the onions in a basin, sprinkle with salt and leave overnight. Rinse the onions under the cold tap. Boil the spices, sugar and vinegar for 5 minutes. Add the onions and bring back to boiling point. Pack the onions into jars and pour vinegar in to completely cover. Leave to cool and screw the lids down. You can pickle cucumber in the same way.

Date and Apple Chutney

This makes a delicious sweet chutney which children like very much. Mine have it with sausages and beefburgers as a change from tomato sauce.

900g (2 lb) apples
450g (1 lb) dates
50g (2 oz) salt
450g (1 lb) tomatoes
825ml (1½ pt.) vinegar
900g (2 lb) demerara sugar
450g (1 lb) onions
25g (1 oz.) ground ginger
1 dessertspoonful mustard
A little paprika

Chop dates and apples. Boil to a pulp in vinegar. Add the other ingredients, and boil for 10 minutes. Pot and seal.

Green Tomato Chutney

A good way of using up all the tomatoes that don't ripen by the end of the season.

1125g (2½ lb) green tomatoes
1 large onion
450g (1 lb) raisins
12g (½ oz.) mustard
Salt and cayenne
900g (2 lb) apples
2 cloves garlic
225g (8 oz.) brown sugar

225g (8 oz.) dates
1 litres (1 quart) vinegar

Chop the tomatoes, apples and onion and boil to a pulp with the vinegar and other ingredients.

Jam Making

Again, save jars, preferably with plastic screw tops. Make your own labels. Cut circles from greaseproof to go over the jam in the pot, and circles from cellophane or plastic bags to seal. You have of course been saving elastic bands. So there is no need to buy special packets of jam pot covers and labels.

Marrow Jam

(Use an old marrow for this. Peel, remove seeds and chop.)
1350g (3 lb) marrow
1575g (3½ lb) sugar
A piece of whole ginger
2 lemons

Put the marrow into a bowl and add the sugar. Leave overnight. Peel the lemons. Squeeze and strain the juice. Tie the ginger in a piece of cloth. Put all the ingredients into a pan and boil gently for 3 hours or so. Test on a cold plate to see if it is setting.

Blackberry and Apple Jelly

900g (2 lb) blackberries
900g (2 lb) apples
Sugar

Wash the apples and cut them into pieces. There is no need to core them. Wash the blackberries. Put both into a preserving pan and cover with water. Boil for 20 minutes, stirring from time to time. Put a large piece of cloth (an old sheet or pillow case) over a bowl and ladle the fruit and juice into it. Gather up the ends of the cloth and tie with string. Leave to drip. Measure the juice in pints and return to pan with 550g (1¼ lb) sugar to every pint. Boil for a few minutes. Then put into jars and seal.

Carrot Marmalade

1350g (3 lb) carrots
1350g (3 lb) sugar
6 lemons
100g (4 oz.) almonds

Use young carrots. Wash and scrape them. Mince. Cover with water and cook until tender, then press through a sieve. Add the sugar, grated lemon rind and juice and simmer for half an hour until thick and clear. Add almonds and put into jars and seal.

Lemon Curd

2 eggs
50g (2 oz.) butter
2 lemons
175g (6 oz.) sugar

Put the sugar into a bowl, squeeze the lemon into it, add the butter and beaten eggs and put the bowl over boiling water. Stir until it thickens, then put into jars.

Parsley Honey

150g (5 oz.) parsley, including stalks
825ml (1½ pt.) water
450g (1 lb) sugar
½ teaspoonful vinegar

Wash and chop the parsley. Boil with the water until it reduces to 1 pt. Strain off the liquid, add the sugar and boil for about half an hour or until syrupy. Add the vinegar. It will have set next day and tastes a little like heather honey. Keep it in the fridge because it doesn't last as long as other jams.

Crab Apple Jelly

Collect as many crab apples as you can. Wash them, remove the stalks and cut out any marks. Put into a pan and cover with water. Boil until soft and mash with a potato masher.

Strain as for Blackberry and Apple Jelly. Do not squeeze the bag. Measure juice, allow 450g (1 lb) sugar to each pint and boil until it reaches the setting stage.

If you keep your eyes open when you're in the country you will find crab apples, blackberries, elderberries and other fruits for free. I'm not telling you where I get my crab apples, but regularly every autumn we go to a famous London open space and the world and his wife walk by while we collect our jam ration.

Wine Making

It is very easy to make wine, and you don't need very much equipment. I simply have some gallon jars (they used to contain cider and you can buy them cheaply at an off-licence), a funnel, a length of tubing, sterilizing tablets and some airlocks. Before I had saved up for the airlocks I used a circle of plastic bag and an elastic band. This keeps the bacteria and dust out of your fermenting wine, and allows the gases to escape during the fermentation process.

Another thing to remember in wine making is never to let metal come in contact with your wine – always use plastic, glass or wooden utensils, well sterilized. It is better to use clear or natural plastic, as coloured can taint the wine a little.

I started off with a beginner's wine-making kit from a wine-making store, and that told me all I needed to known. So I made my first gallon of wine from a quart of grape juice and the yeast that was in the kit. It was so successful that I went on to try other prepared grape juices, and then to make my own wine from other ingredients.

There isn't room here to give you details of how to make wine from all manner of fruits, vegetables, flowers, even jam and tinned fruit, but when you have tried these recipes I'm sure you'll want to buy one of the numerous books on the subject.

Tea wine is one of the cheapest to make, and mine turns out like a pale, medium sherry. But it has such potency that it should be consumed carefully. You will find that the wine you make is often of greater alcoholic content than any you buy in the shops, and the same applies to home-made beer.

Tea Wine

4 litres (8 pt.) cold tea
900g (2 lb) sugar
25g (1 oz.) yeast
450g (1 lb) chopped raisins

1 orange
1 lemon

Make the tea freshly. Chop up the raisins, mix with the tea and the peel and juice from the fruit. Add the yeast. (I have made this most successfully with ordinary dried yeast, but it is best to buy special all-purpose wine yeast.) Do this mixing in a sterilized plastic bucket, and leave to ferment for 7 days, covered closely with a clean cloth or sheet of plastic. Strain off the solids, add the sugar and pour the liquid into your sterilized gallon jar. Fit the airlock and leave to ferment until it stops sending bubbles through the airlock.

It is best to 'stabilize' the wine with wine stabilizer, after filtering or racking (drawing the clear liquid off through a tube), and bottling in sterilized bottles with sterilized corks.

You can sterilize by dissolving a Campden Tablet in warm water, and you can use this sterilizing liquid several times over.

Elderflower Wine
550ml (1 pt.) elderflowers (pressed down)
225g (8 oz.) chopped raisins
1350g (3 lb) sugar
4·5 litres (1 gallon) water
Rind and juice of 2 lemons and 1 orange
½ cupful cold tea
25g (1 oz.) yeast

Snip the florets off the stalks. Don't use the stalks or green parts or your wine will be bitter. Put the flowers into a bucket and pour boiling water on to them. Cover the bucket and give a stir occasionally during the next three days. Strain the liquid off and mix with the other ingredients. Leave for a week. Strain again and then put into your gallon jar with fermentation lock.

Leave until it stops fermenting, then rack off the clear wine. Leave for another three months, rack again and bottle. It is best to leave this wine to mature for a year.

Carrot Wine
This is a really economical wine to make. You only use the juice from the carrots, so you can put them in stews, serve them up

with the meal or make them into soup.

4·5 litres (1 gallon) water
1625g ($3\frac{1}{2}$ lb) sugar
2 oranges
2 lemons
2700g (6 lb) carrots
25g (1 oz.) yeast

Scrub the carrots and bring to the boil in the water. Simmer until tender. Put the sugar, sliced oranges and lemons into a bucket, pour the hot carrot water over them and stir until the sugar is dissolved. Cool to lukewarm and add the yeast.

Cover the bucket and ferment for a fortnight, then strain into a gallon jar with airlock. Leave to finish fermentation, then rack off and stabilize.

Points to Remember

1. Make sure all your equipment is sterilized.
2. Add yeast when liquid is lukewarm not hot, or you will kill it.
3. Cover closely or use an airlock, or the Vinegar Bug could get in and spoil it.
4. Stabilize the wine and use corks, never screwtops.
5. While the fermenting is going on, the jars should be in a temperature of around 22°C/70°F.
6. Finished wine should be stored in a low temperature, but not allowed to freeze.
7. I have always just sprinkled the yeast into the liquid, but some people like to make a starter bottle, adding the yeast to a little of the liquid, until it starts to froth and then putting it into the wine.
8. Do not use metal containers, or old stone jars. There might be lead in the glaze which would be bad for the wine, and you. Plastic or glass is best. Gallon containers are easiest to manage. Some friends of mine made wine in a ten-gallon carboy. *She* knocked it with the vacuum cleaner, and the result was a flood of wine which pushed up the woodblock flooring.

Freezing

If you haven't got one already, try to save up for a small freezer. I find the type with shelves easy to cope with, as it doesn't mean standing on your head to find things, and it is easy to rotate your stock.

Some people who eat a lot of meat find making an arrangement with a butcher a good way of cutting their meat bill. But if you're not in the habit of eating half a pig, don't buy one.

I use my freezer to store other people's gluts of vegetables and fruit, and to stock up with my own cooked meals – like soups, cakes, bread, casseroles, pizza, flans, and so on. If you do this it means you can cook in bulk, saving preparation time, oven heat and clearing-up time. If you don't feel like cooking some days, or have some big important job to do, like decorating or sorting out the back yard, you have food on hand.

You will need strong plastic bags, and paper-covered wire ties, so save them whenever they come into your home. You can use them over and over again. I bought a box of six tart plates and these I wash and re-use. If you are lucky enough to have a Chinese carry-out meal, save the foil dishes. They are perfect for such things as small stews and shepherds pie. Also save plastic boxes with lids. There is absolutely no need to spend a fortune on packing materials for your freezing, and really no need to buy a load of stuff from the freezer market. The only thing I have ever bought there is ice-cream, turkey out of season and 10-lb boxes of peas. I did once buy some cheap mince, but it turned out to be of very inferior quality, which I couldn't see in its frozen-solid state. I found a butcher who sold better quality at the same price, so now I buy it fresh, pack it myself and freeze it. My freezer is also useful for perishable bargains from the supermarket, like butter, margarine, lard, and cheese when on special offer.

It is also useful for the cat's dinners. I buy a few pounds of cheap fish, cook it up and freeze it in individual packs. I hate the smell of cat fish boiling, so that only happens occasionally now. I find it cheaper to feed the cat this way than to buy tins of food. Anyway, she says they have changed the recipes so much that she won't eat it. And you can't force a cat to eat anything! You might like to make up your own cat's food recipe, with offal and fish, mixed.

Before I had a freezer I had to sadly decline the gluts of fruit offered by country friends. We could only eat so much of one fruit or another before the family went on strike, but now I can prepare and freeze everything I'm offered and serve it up at intervals during the winter months.

Last Christmas it didn't matter that the family didn't want any more from my cauldron of turkey soup. I froze it, and we enjoyed it in March. My father makes soup by the gallon, packs it in individual half pints and so has a constant supply of all flavours to eat with bread and cheese at lunch time.

What Not to freeze

Custard, bananas, cream, eggs, jelly, mayonnaise, melons, milk, salad vegetables, yogurt. None of these will look the same when you thaw them. They will discolour, go black, or collapse or separate.

Fruit

The simplest way to prepare fruit for the freezer is to peel, core and slice it, or wash and de-stone it, and cook it in slightly sweetened water for a few minutes. Then pour it into plastic bags. Put these into square containers to freeze. Remove them from the containers and you have easily-stored blocks.

Thaw overnight before using. You can keep fruit prepared like this for a year in the freezer.

Vegetables

All vegetables must be cooked in boiling water for a few minutes before being stored in bags in the freezer. The easiest way to do this is to put 450g (1 lb) of vegetables into a wire basket and lower this into a big pan of boiling water for the required time. Then cool under the cold tap, drain and pack. Divide into 225g (8 oz.) packs, or whatever is the most manageable for you to use.

The various vegetables require different 'blanching' (that means boiling) times to keep them at their best. Here are the preparation details and blanching times for some common vegetables:

	Preparation	*Blanching Time*
Broad beans	Shell them	3 minutes
Brussels sprouts	Trim, wash	4 minutes
Broccoli	Trim stalks, wash	3 minutes
Cabbage	Wash and shred	$1\frac{1}{2}$ minutes
Carrots	Scrub, trim	5 minutes
Cauliflower	Break into sprigs, wash	3 minutes
Corn on the cob	Remove husk and silk	8 minutes
French beans	Wash, trim and slice	2 minutes
Leeks	Slice	1 minute
Peas	Shell	2 minutes
Root vegetables	Peel and dice	2 minutes
Spinach	Trim, wash	2 minutes
Mushrooms	Fry for one minute in oil	

Potatoes can be frozen after boiling, roasting or mashing.
Chips should be fried for 4 minutes, but not browned, before freezing.
Tomatoes can be puréed or packed in bags as they are, but the whole ones will collapse when they thaw. They can then be used in soups, sauces, stews.

Freezing Your Own Cooking

You can freeze cakes, bread, buns, rolls, pies, stews, flans, puddings and so on very simply. Just let them cool and then pack into plastic bags. Exclude as much air as possible before sealing. You may like to put stew in a plastic bag in your favourite casserole, freeze it like that and then take it out of the casserole. This means you have a shape that fits your dish when you come to use it.

Don't leave bread in the freezer for longer than a month, as the crust separates from the inside, but everything else will remain intact for 3 months at least. After that it will be perfectly okay to eat, but may deteriorate in colour and texture.

You can freeze small portions of parsley, sage, thyme, mint or any other herbs you might otherwise have dried. When you take the bag out of the freezer there is no chopping involved. Just crush the bag and the frozen sprigs fall to pieces ready to flavour your cooking. You may find the flavour stronger, so go carefully.

Always Remember

1. To de-frost your freezer regularly, as recommended in the handbook you were given with it.
2. Label everything with what it is and when it was frozen.
3. Never re-freeze thawed food.
4. Wrap well to avoid 'freezer burn' – small white or grey patches which spoil the look of your food.

When you have been playing with your freezer for a while, I am sure you'll become so enthusiastic you'll want to buy a complete book on the subject.

9

Let's Be Entertaining

If you are homemaking on a tight budget you can seldom afford to eat out, let alone treat your friends, so in order to have a social life you will be entertaining at home.

Don't waste any more time, effort and money on people you don't really like. You can stop the silly ping-pong game of: 'We must have them to dinner. They invited us last month.' Pay them back, if your conscience hurts, but make an excuse when they invite you again. If it is business, try to do the entertaining in business hours, on your expense account.

Remember, your real friends have come to see *you*, and if the food is tasty, nourishing and attractively presented, it doesn't have to be expensive. Lots of people only pretend to like snails, caviar and oysters anyway!

Your friends are probably equally broke, and you could start a nice bit of give and take if you offer to bring the dessert next time they invite you over. Then they will bring one of their special recipes when they come to you. This is especially useful if you're working and also have children to see to, as you end up with less work to do towards your dinner party. Don't let your guests wash up, or they'll expect you to return the chore!

Drink

Serve cider or your own wine, and this will cut costs in the drinks section. Give up buying expensive drinks like sherry, gin, whisky and so on. Serve a small glass of wine when your guests arrive, and have plenty of soft drinks like lemon and tomato juice. Many women prefer not to drink 'shorts' anyway – if they care about their complexion and nervous system. And with so much stress on drinking and driving it isn't fair to get the driver plastered. If your friends come on bikes, the same applies, as bikes behave badly after one drink too many. I had a bike once that gravitated towards thorn hedges after just one glass of cider.

Atmosphere

Pleasant background music (you can borrow records and cassettes from the library), low lights, and telling your girl friends you are planning to wear a long dress, all contribute towards a pleasant atmosphere. Candlelight is flattering, and if you haven't had time to dust, no one is going to know about it.

Set the table prettily. I've given up buying paper napkins as part of my economy campaign. You can easily make some from cotton material. Mine match the curtains and go into the weekly wash. If you like to serve pastries on a paper doily, don't buy these either. Make your own, or get the children to by folding and cutting thin plain paper.

Getting Ready

Try to prepare as much of the meal as possible the night before, so that you have time to get yourself ready. There's nothing worse than being caught with your hair in rollers, or flapping your arms about to dry your nail varnish as the guests arrive.

Children enjoy laying the table to look extra special, and mine actually fight for the privilege. If they do it for you, you only need to give it a quick check over to remove anything really extraordinary in the way of decoration. My youngest son had a passion for putting a large vase of very dusty feathers in the middle of the table, but I was able to remove them diplomatically, saying they were so tall that the guests would have to peer round them. Remember that, your flower decoration should not be more than 15cm (6 inches) high.

The Food

It's a good idea to keep a notebook and write down the dishes you

'I've laid the table, Mum!'.

have served to various friends. I realized this was essential when I said to one of my girl friends: 'I can't remember whether you've had lasagne before?' and she said, very kindly: 'Your lasagne is *always* very good, Jo.'

If you don't do this, you may fall into the habit of thinking: Janet and John are definitely Coq au Vin people, Beryl is a pasta person, and of course Alastair is a Kipper Paté type, whereas Brenda is quite obviously salad and lentil cutlet.

Here are some of our favourite dishes for supper parties. None is wildly expensive, and they always go down well.

For Starters

Cucumber Vichyssoise

450g (1 lb) potatoes
1 cucumber
50g (2 oz.) margarine
1 small onion
1 litres (2 pt.) chicken stock (your own, naturally)
150ml ($\frac{1}{4}$ pt.) top of the milk
Salt and pepper

Peel the potatoes and onion and chop up into small pieces. Chop up the unpeeled cucumber. Melt the margarine, add the vegetables and cook gently with the lid on the pan for 10 minutes, shaking occasionally. Add the stock and cook until all is tender. Put through a sieve. Stir in the top of the milk and seasoning. Chill. Serve with a sprinkling of chives or parsley for decoration.

Taramasalata

3 thick slices white bread
Milk
75g (3 oz.) smoked cod's roe
1 clove garlic
2 tablespoonsful grated onion
Juice of a lemon
4 tablespoonsful oil

Cut the crusts from the bread, and soak it in a little milk. Remove the skins from the roes and pound them in a bowl until smooth. Add the soaked bread, squeezed dry, the garlic and onion and pound together again. Add the lemon juice and oil. Mix to a creamy consistency. Serve with thin toast.

Chicken Liver Paté

50g (2 oz.) margarine
1 small chopped onion
2 bay leaves
Pinch of dried thyme
450g (1 lb) chicken livers
Salt and pepper

Gently fry the onion, bay leaves and thyme in the margarine.

Clean the chicken livers and cut them up, add them to the pan and simmer for a few minutes until cooked. Remove bay leaves. Mash the livers up and put through a sieve. Season and put into an attractive dish. Garnish with parsley and serve with thin slices of toast or French bread (your own).

The Main Course

Chicken is good value, and often turkey is an even better bargain if you buy it out of season. If you have a freezer it's worth looking around for cut-price bargains directly after Christmas and Easter to keep for later. You can cook either in many delicious ways. Here are a few recipes for dinner parties – or Sunday lunch. Each makes 4 adult portions.

Chicken Veronique

Get the butcher to joint a roasting chicken for you, or buy four joints. Simmer the quarters in seasoned stock until tender. Cool and remove the flesh from the bones and put in an ovenproof dish.

Melt 50g (2 oz.) margarine and stir in 50g (2 oz.) flour. Gradually add 550ml (1 pt.) chicken stock (or you could use half white wine – your own, of course – and half stock. Season. Boil to thicken. Add 150ml ($\frac{1}{4}$ pt.) top of the milk and 100g (4 oz.) green grapes. Pour over the chicken and heat through.

Serve with boiled rice, into which you have stirred a selection of diced vegetables – cooked carrot, peas, green pepper, tomato, corn. Don't buy a packet of frozen mixed vegetables . It's cheaper to mix your own.

Chicken in Garlic Cream

Cook the chicken as for Chicken Veronique. Crush a clove of garlic and mix with 275ml ($\frac{1}{2}$ pt.) cream. Pour over the chicken and serve cold with cold rice (again with mixed vegetables stirred in if you like). You can use 150ml ($\frac{1}{4}$ pt.) thick cream, and 150ml ($\frac{1}{4}$ pt.) top of the milk.

Indian Chicken Pilau

Allow one chicken joint per person and put them in a roasting tin with 2 tablespoonsful dripping. Sprinkle the joints with a tablespoonful of curry powder (shared between them all) and roast at gas mark 5, 375°F/190°C, for about half an hour, basting occasionally.

I use a paella pan, which means I can cook the chicken, then the rice, and serve the completed dish in the original pan. Only one dish to wash!

Remove the joints from the dripping and put to one side.

Prepare the rice bed as follows:

225g (½ lb) onion sliced into rings
450g (1 lb) long-grain rice, rinsed under the tap
1 teaspoonful turmeric
100g (4 oz.) raisins
Handful of nuts (cashew or unsalted peanuts...
8 cardomom seeds
2 bay leaves
Salt and pepper

Fry the onion rings in the curry-flavoured dripping until soft. Add the rice. Measure it by the cupful, and add 2 cups water for each cup of rice. Stir in all the other ingredients. Bring to the boil and simmer gently with the lid on until the rice has absorbed all the liquid. I find it useful to cook it gently in the oven, then it doesn't stick to the pan and I'm free to chat to my guests. Place chicken joints on top of the rice and serve. You can if you like add pieces of red pepper and tomato to make it more colourful.

Cheese is cheap and yet can be the main ingredient of many dishes suitable for supper parties. It can also be used to eke out a small amount of meat.

Moussaka

50g (2 oz.) margarine
450g (1 lb) potatoes (cooked and sliced)
2 sliced onions
2 sliced tomatoes
225g (8 oz.) cooked lamb (or mince)
Salt and pepper
25g (1 oz.) flour
275ml (½ pt.) milk and water)
150g (5 oz.) cheese

Melt half the margarine and fry the potatoes lightly. Place in a shallow ovenproof dish. Fry the onions and tomatoes until soft. Add the lamb and seasoning and pour over the potatoes. Make a white sauce with the remaining butter and the flour and milk. Add half the cheese and season. Pour the sauce over the meat mixture. Sprinkle with the rest of the cheese. Bake at gas mark 5, 375°F/200°C, for 25 minutes until golden brown.

Pizza and Quiche are ideal dishes for a buffet party, served with a bowl of salad. You'll find recipes for these in Chapter 4.

Salad does not mean just lettuce, cucumber and tomato. You can put almost any fruit or vegetable into it. If you use white cabbage or the heart of any other cabbage, shred it and leave it in cold water for a few hours. This gets rid of the (to put it politely) 'gassy' juices.

You can use any of the following to make a really interesting salad, and once you are on the wavelength you'll think of many more.

Green: Lettuce, cabbage, celery, endive, cucumber, grapes, green pepper, green apple, onion sprouts, peas, beans, parsley.

Red: Tomato, diced beetroot, red apple, radish, red pepper.

Yellow: Corn, golden apple, pear, pineapple, carrot, peach, apricot, grated swede.

Brown: Dates, nuts, sultanas, raisins.

White: Nuts, chicory, onion, bean shoots, mushrooms, banana, grated parsnip, cooked potato.

Don't buy salad cream or mayonnaise, and certainly do not buy ready-mixed French dressing. Make your own.

French Dressing

Clove of garlic or a little chopped onion or chives
Pepper and salt
2 teaspoonsful sugar
1 teaspoonful mustard
3 tablespoonsful vinegar
5 tablespoonsful corn or groundnut oil

Crush the garlic, if you want to include it, and put all the ingredients into a screwtop jar. Shake the jar thoroughly until well blended. You can keep this in the fridge for ages.

Mayonnaise

2 egg yolks
½ teaspoonful dry mustard
¼ teaspoonful salt
¼ teaspoonful sugar
Pepper
275ml (½ pt.) oil
2 tablespoonsful lemon juice
(or 1 tablespoonful lemon and 1 tablespoonful wine vinegar)

Put the egg yolks into a deep bowl with the mustard, salt, sugar, and pepper. Add the oil drop by drop, beating with a wooden spoon. When half the oil has been added, beat in 1 teaspoonful lemon juice. Beat well. Add the rest of the oil, in dribbles, then the last of the lemon juice (or vinegar).

Delicious Desserts

Orange Mousse or Crême Caramel are light finishes to a meal, but if the first courses have not been particularly substantial, you might like to serve Cheese Cake.

Fresh fruit salad is the easiest thing to make. Just dissolve a dessertspoonful of sugar in 150ml (¼ pt.) water, let it cool and then add any fruit you have, cut up. Leave to soak in the juice for a while before serving. You could use orange or lemon squash instead of the sugar and water syrup.

Orange Mousse

4 tablespoonsful cold water
1 rounded tablespoonful powdered gelatine
3 eggs
75g (3 oz.) caster sugar
3 medium-sized oranges

This is very light, fluffy and refreshing. Put the cold water into a pan, sprinkle gelatine over it and leave to soak for 5 minutes, then heat (without boiling) until the gelatine has dissolved. Remove from heat.

Separate the egg yolks and whites into two basins. Add half

the sugar and the grated rind of one orange to the yolks. Whisk until light and thick. Squeeze the juice from the three oranges, strain and add to the gelatine, then whisk this mixture into the egg yolks. Put to chill.

Whisk egg whites until stiff, add the rest of the sugar, whisk again until stiff. Fold into orange mixture. Chill.

Crême Caramel

For the topping:

100g (4 oz.) caster sugar
150ml ($\frac{1}{4}$ pt.) water

For the crême:

25g (1 oz.) caster sugar
3 eggs
550ml (1 pt.) milk
Vanilla essence

Dissolve the sugar in the water over a gentle heat. Bring to the boil and cook until golden brown. Pour into 5 or 6 coffee cups or moulds.

Beat the eggs with the sugar. Heat the milk until it is almost boiling and pour it on to the eggs, stirring all the time. Add a few drops of vanilla. Strain through a sieve and divide between the cups or moulds.

Stand the cups in a baking tin with water coming half way up and bake at gas mark 3, 325°F/190°C, for about three-quarters of an hour, or until set. Serve hot or cold, turned out into individual dishes.

Cheese Cake

Pastry case:

100g (4 oz.) plain flour
Pinch of salt
25g (1 oz.) margarine
25g (1 oz.) lard
Water to mix

For the filling:

225g (8 oz.) cream cheese
25g (1 oz.) melted butter

25g (1 oz.) sultanas or currants
50g (2 oz.) caster sugar
1 teaspoonful finely grated lemon rind
2 drops vanilla essence
1 beaten egg

I have made this most successfully in the summer using cream cheese made from milk that has gone sour (see Chapter 3).

Sift the flour and salt, mix in the fats with your finger tips. Add 2 tablespoonsful water. Roll out two-thirds of this pastry and line an 20cm (8 inch) flan tin. Prick with a fork. Keep the rest of the pastry for decoration.

Mix the filling ingredients together, starting at the top of the list. Pour into flan case. Roll out the rest of the pastry and cut into thin strips. Make a lattice pattern on top of the filling.

Bake at gas mark 6, 400°F/200°C, for about thirty minutes or until the filling is set and very pale brown.

Entertaining a Crowd

Of course you can always give them wine and cheese, but another idea is to have plates piled high with hot mini-Cornish pasties with various fillings. You'll find ideas for them in my chapter on 'Kid's Stuff'. This is a much cheaper way than cheese.

10

Especially for Working Mums

First of all, if you are a working mum, stop feeling guilty about it. If you have to work, you have to work, and if you can organize your cooking, shopping and housework and get it done during the weekday evenings, you can make sure you spend the weekend doing things with your children, or doing something for yourself. Good for them, and good for you. One way to take the pressure off and give you an occasional free day at the weekend is to arrange Swoppachild with a friend. That means for me that I have someone else's children for meals, giving her a free day, and she has mine in return. If I'm cooking for three children, I might as well cook for six.

Don't spend your hard-earned money on expensive tinned, frozen and packaged foods. If you spend two evenings a week doing the baking, and preparing casseroles, pies and so on, you will save money, and you will be feeding your family on good, nourishing food without those strange 'additives' which have to be used when food is factory processed.

In order to find the time to 'make it – not buy it', you will need some sort of time-table, organized around the needs of your own particular family, and yourself. Maybe there's a baby to be collected from nursery or baby-minder, urgently needing a plate of cereal and a bottle, young children to feed and get to bed with a soothing story, or a husband who needs feeding early because he's going to his evening class.

At present my children eat about six o'clock in order to have baths and be in bed at a reasonable time. I prefer to eat at eight-thirty. I don't go to evening classes, but I have my Italian course on cassettes, so I'm having some of my tuition while I'm working in the kitchen.

Sorry, you have to unhook yourself from the television if you're going to be an economical cook, but the radio still has a lot going for it – plays, talks, music, discussion programmes and so on.

Baking Ahead

You will know roughly how many loaves, cakes and biscuits you get through in a week, so cook this batch one evening a week. This is my time-table for Thursday baking night. But I think it is important to be elastic. Obviously if friends drop in, or I'm feeling under the weather, I switch it to another night.

I work full-time and I switch off the office as I leave the building. Walking the half mile from the station, I try to think happy thoughts, and don't start any self-pitying saga about all the work I've got to do. The only thing I have to do on that walk home is breathe the fresh air, look at the trees and be thankful I have a home and kids to go to. I know my mood influences the tone for the evening. I'm not the only one who has had a hard day. Kids are under pressure at school, and the last thing they want is their mother coming in all tensed up.

6.00 Arrive home. Have a cup of coffee and a sit down. This is most important! Also gives the kids time to tell me anything urgent and produce one of those dozens of notes telling you what is happening or not happening at school.

6.15 Feed 3 school-age children. They have had a good lunch, at school, so this is probably soup and home-made bread, and something like pizza and salad and fresh fruit.

6.30 Prepare dough for bread and leave to rise. Children clear table and wash up unless they have something urgent to do.

7.00 Mix up ingredients for cake and weekly batch of biscuits. You can cut them in squares instead of rounds, for speed. That saves collecting up the offcuts and re-rolling. Also saves you wondering what to do with the tiny bits of leftover pastry. If I am doing rounds, I make the last bits into a ball and just squash it into a round. Put cake in middle of oven and biscuits at top.

7.30 Dough has risen. Knead it. Put it in tins and leave to rise for 10 minutes. Biscuits are now ready.

8.00 Put dough in oven. Cake is usually done by now. Chivvy kids to bed, kiss them, and tuck them in tightly.

8.30 Grown-ups' supper. Same as the children had.

9.00 Take bread out of oven.

If you are working, you don't want to spend time serving meals to different members of the family all through the evening to fit in with their comings and goings. I find that saying first supper is at 6.15 and second at 8.30 solves the problem. If my older children are at home, they can join whichever sitting suits their life-style. Anyone who comes in at an extraordinary hour has to fend for himself.

My small sons go to sea cadets and have to be seen to the bus when I get in on Wednesday, but that problem is solved by leaving them a packed tea in a sandwich box – sandwiches, cake and fruit. And they get their own milk. If they are hungry when they get in from school at four o'clock they have a bowl of cereal, which saves worrying about them using the breadknife or the stove.

Hungry children can be aggressive or whiney, and I think it is important for them to know that they can help themselves to cereal or cake. Let them know what they can have, and what they can dispense to those equally starving friends of theirs, then you won't find they've raided the larder or fridge and gobbled up something you'd planned to serve for the proper supper.

Main Meal Cooking

On another night during the week, I prepare a number of main dishes: for instance, stew, a pot of mince, a liver casserole. Stew is always improved by being left overnight and re-heated the next day. Leaving it to sit in its own juice breaks down the fibres and can make the toughest meat tender. While you're preparing vegetables for one dish, you might as well do it for three, because it seems to me that the clearing up and washing up after preparing a dish is less time-consuming that way. If you have a member of the family who comes home for lunch, decant some of the casserole, stew or what-have-you into a small individual pot for him to warm up. I suggested this to a working mum who had a teenager who refused to stay for school lunch. She had been spending a fortune on ready-made, frozen, individual meals. She's saving money now.

If I make pastry, I make enough for two or three dishes. This way you can put some away in the freezer or fridge. I make a lot of pizza, quiche and Cornish pasties as these are very useful for suppers or packed lunches.

If I'm making macaroni cheese, I make double the quantity of cheese sauce and store the surplus in a screw top jar in the fridge, where it's ready for cauliflower cheese or perhaps lasagne at the weekend.

We eat a lot of salad (often using cabbage hearts instead of lettuce, and grated carrot and apple when tomatoes are pricey). And giving the kids fresh fruit for dessert saves cooking time and makes sure they get plenty of vitamins. I also make my own mousse and have yogurt on the go most of the time.

If I make crumble topping for stewed fruit, I make double the quantity and store some in a screwtop jar in the fridge.

Sunday Lunch

This is an institution – and who wants to live in an institution. If the weather is fine, I don't want to spend half the precious day slaving over a hot stove and then cleaning greasy utensils, so we often have a one-dish meal, like lasagne or risotto, or take a picnic to the park or out into the country.

I don't bake at weekends in the summer, but it is fun to get the kids in on it during the winter months when the weather may be too cold or wet for excursions or walks.

Shopping

This I try to do mid-week at an early-opening supermarket before going to work. But if your children are old enough there is no reason why they shouldn't take turns to do it after school. They're going to eat the stuff, and it does make them aware of prices and so on. Also they are quite likely to spot bargains and tell you about them. All you have to do is leave a shopping list with what you expect to pay against each item, and the money, of course. In some ways it's better to send kids or husband to do the basic shopping. I know they stick to the list and are less easily tempted than I am.

I shop for fruit and some of the vegetables in the market in my lunch hour about twice a week. So my Saturday shopping trip just means a quick trip to the butcher, and the greengrocer for fresh vegetables.

I try not to end up carrying heavy bags home from work. It is cleverer to distribute the load evenly between two bags, to avoid one arm growing longer than the other.

We always have the milk delivered, and I leave a note for the eggs.

Thinking Ahead

The day starts better, I find, if I have laid the breakfast table the night before, with the kids' cereal, mugs, bowls, sugar, spoons, plates, margarine (in a covered dish), jam or whatever.

Preparation for Cooking

When I start on a session I find it easiest to get all the ingredients out, weigh them, then put the packets back in the cupboards. And I keep the washing-up bowl full of water so that I can put used cooking utensils to soak immediately. My kitchen is so small that if I don't do this I have no room to work!

Sharing the Work

The worst thing you can do for your family is to become a slave and martyr. They won't love you for it. Secretly they'll think you're daft, or an old misery. Or they'll take you for granted and grow up unaware of what it takes to run a home. Then they'll have to learn the hard way, either when they're adjusting to living on their own, sharing a flat, or starting off on marriage.

Particularly if you're working, get everyone to pull their weight. There is a lot of work in running a home, and you shouldn't do it all yourself, or you'll wake up one day to find the fledglings have flown and your house is in order, but you're bored because you haven't had time to cultivate your own interests or develop your

'Sunday morning tea, Mum!'

own talents.

It's best to catch them young. Even a small child can do all sorts of useful things to help towards the smooth running of the home. Start them off putting out the rubbish and the milk bottles. Slightly older and they can lay and clear tables and help with the washing up. That's a useful time for mum-daughter, mum-son, dad-daughter, dad-son chats about their lives and problems with Sir or Miss at school. And in a large family it may be one of the few times for a one-to-one conversation. Information and thoughts are more naturally exchanged when one person is washing up and the other is drying up, and there's nothing forced about the conversation usually.

However, I do remember at thirteen drying up while my father washed up, and he finally got around to trying to tell me about the birds and the bees. He cleared his throat and said: 'Now, Josie. There are probably a few things you would like to know about – um – the Facts of Life.' I was dying to get filled in, but he was obviously so embarrassed that I shone another glass and tried to put him at his ease: 'That's okay, Pop, I know absolutely all there is to know.' He swallowed, looked worried, and tried to get the burnt off the outside of a saucepan that had never been attacked before.

Some parents say they just can't get their children to help. I've found that praise works wonders, and if you say to a child: 'I really don't know how I'd manage without your help,' it makes him even more keen to please. Of course they don't manage to do everything perfectly, but they improve, just as we did. I received a pot of lukewarm tea with the sugar and milk already mixed up in it from my eight-year-old son recently, but he's got the hang of it all now. I just have to train him not to arrive with it at crack of dawn while I'm trying to have a Sunday lie-in!

Under the new sexual discrimination act you're not supposed to discriminate between 'persons'. In fact you are doing your sons a favour if you teach them simple cookery. You don't want them to go out into the big world to live on baked beans and packet curries. They'll make more friends if they can entertain in their bed-sits with such simple and economical dishes as Spaghetti Bolognese.

And later on, your daughter-in-law will not be able to complain that your son is handless, untrained and unaware. But don't make him *too* clever – or she might be unable to show off her cookery to him.

If you are working, make out a list of priorities. To me they are in this order – my health, seeing everyone eats properly. Last on the list comes trying to keep up with the Jones's and their spotless house. The atmosphere is more important than worrying about dust on the piano. Anyway, if you keep enough things on it, there won't be room for dust!

Index